IRRATIONAL
LOYALTY

BUILDING A BRAND THAT
THRIVES IN TURBULENT TIMES

DEB GABOR

Author of *Branding Is Sex*

LIONCREST
PUBLISHING

IRRATIONAL LOYALTY

Building a Brand That Thrives in Turbulent Times

ISBN   978-1-5445-1362-1 *Paperback*
       978-1-5445-1361-4 *Ebook*

I dedicate this book to the people behind the best brands in the world: the thoughtful stewards of brand promises, relationships, and experiences that attract—and hold dearly in their hearts—legions of irrationally loyal fans.

CONTENTS

INTRODUCTION

Can you imagine a brand that literally kills three of its customers (as in *dead*), yet somehow the (surviving) customers remain loyal and devoted to the company and its products?

This is not a rhetorical question. It really happened. It's an incredible story of a brand that suffered a massive branding disaster but handled it the right way and came out stronger on the other side.

If you're from the Lone Star State, you have heard of Blue Bell ice cream. Blue Bell Creameries has been satisfying Texans' sweet tooths for more than a century. Founded in 1907, the company expanded into dozens of midwestern and southern states, bringing their addictive flavors—such as Moo-llennium Crunch, Cookie Two-Step, and my favorite, Peppermint Bark—to millions of loyal customers. The company earned a reputation for producing a great product at a fair price and treating its employees like family.

In 2015, disaster struck. Five Blue Bell customers came down with cases of the infectious foodborne disease, listeria, linked directly to contaminated Blue Bell ice cream. Three people died.

The company responded immediately by issuing the first product recall in its 108-year history. They removed eight million gallons of ice cream from store shelves and disposed of it in a sanitary landfill. Then management closed most of the company's manufacturing operations and distribution centers for decontamination and cleaning.

The situation lasted for months and threatened to bankrupt Blue Bell. Nevertheless, true to its brand promise and reputation, Blue Bell continued to pay its employees. The company had to secure a $125 million loan to pay for salaries during the shutdown and for the continued cleanup operation. Since Blue Bell was a major employer in its hometown of Brenham, customers throughout Texas who loved the brand followed the evolving saga as it played out on the local news.

While Blue Bell fought its way back from being deeply in

debt and on the brink of bankruptcy, people noticed that the company put its employees and its customers' safety ahead of profits—ahead of even the survival of the company. In September 2015, when Blue Bell's Homemade Vanilla reappeared on store shelves, customers lined up to buy it—literally out the door, around the corner, and down the street—at grocery stores across Texas. It was like they were waiting in line for hot concert tickets.

For many months, as manufacturing slowly ramped up again, the only flavor available was vanilla. Not everyone likes vanilla. But loyal customers lined up to buy it anyway, just to support Blue Bell, whether they intended to eat it or not.

That is an example of irrational loyalty.

IRRATIONAL LOYALTY

Irrational loyalty exists when customers are so dedicated to a certain brand that their lives would be diminished if that product disappeared. Irrational loyalty means customers wouldn't even consider using an alternative brand; they'd feel like they were *cheating*. The way brands build irrational loyalty among their customers is by bonding emotionally.

EMOTIONAL BONDS

Blue Bell had forged deep emotional relationships with its

customers and employees by building up positive brand equity and goodwill. That's how they were able to endure and overcome such a horrifying tragedy. There are things you can do in the creation, management, and leadership of your own brand to ensure that you build a solid emotional bond with your customers.

Similarly, as with relationships between people, you form the strongest bonds when there's alignment of values and beliefs. At the foundation of the relationship there is inherent trust and accountability, which create an emotional bond. If there is a strong enough emotional bond, the relationship can survive when someone screws up.

Blue Bell Creameries *literally killed some of its customers.* But because of the company's commitment to its brand promise, it acted in a way consistent with the Blue Bell brand. When disaster struck, Blue Bell lived up to its values. As a result, the loyalty that customers felt to the brand strengthened and grew into irrational loyalty, solidifying the company's standing in the marketplace and ensuring the brand's continued survival for decades to come.

Can your brand survive a disaster like that?

BRANDS SCREW UP ALL THE TIME

In today's world, there are more opportunities for brands to screw up publicly than ever before. News and information travel at the speed of broadband. Anything and everything you do as a brand can be captured on smartphone video, streamed across the globe in a matter of minutes, and memorialized for eternity on Facebook and Twitter. And you have no control over it. Just ask United Airlines. (We'll talk about them as a cautionary tale later in the book.)

Every company and every brand eventually will get into hot water. It is unavoidable. It may not even be your fault. Many brand crises are external; they come from unforeseen outside forces. For example, the National Football League had no idea Colin Kaepernick would cause a national controversy when he decided to kneel during the National Anthem. The NFL never saw it coming. But the branding crisis it caused landed squarely in the NFL's lap. They had to deal with it.

The question is not whether your brand will eventually face controversy or calamity. The question is how to react when it happens. The key is to always respond in accordance with your brand promise.

When Hurricane Harvey flooded large parts of Texas, Bass Pro Shops reacted with their brand promise in mind.

They provided more than eighty bass boats to help in the search, recovery, and relief efforts. They also donated survival supplies and snacks like beef jerky and bottled water for first responders and rescue crews.

As we will discuss in the coming chapters, a crisis can be the best time to reinforce your brand promise and your commitment to your customers. Unfortunately, it's also a time when many brands drop the ball and suffer because of a botched strategy.

BRANDING IS SEX GETS INTO A COMMITTED RELATIONSHIP

All brands want to enjoy the condition of irrational loyalty from their customers, just like Blue Bell. In my previous book, *Branding Is Sex: Get Your Customers Laid and Sell the Hell Out of Anything*, I gave concrete, nuts-and-bolts, how-to advice to help brands build that kind of loyalty. This book picks up where that book left off.

BIS used the analogy of the early stages of a romantic relationship to illustrate the basics of branding. It included attracting and courting customers, sealing the deal, and building the emotional bonds that lead to loyalty. This second book continues that relationship theme by taking romance to the logical next step—actually being in a committed relationship with your customer for the long term.

Now the honeymoon is over and the initial shine of courtship has dulled, replaced with the day-to-day realities of life together and all its ups and downs. One of the partners in the relationship has traded in the rose-colored glasses for a worn-out pair of sweatpants and bunny slippers, and started peeing with the bathroom door wide open. The other partner comes to bed covered in face cream and wearing their fluffiest, most comfortable pajamas. There's comfort, contentment, and trust. But the spark of intrigue and excitement has dimmed a bit. The fog of pheromones has cleared, and you begin to see your partner for who they really are.

The same thing happens with brands. Now that the fun courtship is over, how do brands keep customers satisfied, happy, engaged, and loyal for a lifetime? How can a brand build such a powerful emotional connection with customers that it can weather any storm and overcome any setback?

SURVIVING HEARTBREAK AND BETRAYAL

Just as in relationships between people, brands occasionally break their promise, which can threaten or destroy the entire relationship. This book will explore case studies of major brands like United Airlines, Pepsi, Papa John's, Wells Fargo, and Uber, all of which broke their promise to their customers and suffered for it.

A key question this book will answer is, *can those relationships survive a broken brand promise?* And if so, or if not, why? In the coming chapters, we'll explore how brands can maintain a solid emotional foundation with their customers over the life of a relationship.

This book will dig deeper into what a brand promise is. We'll examine the relationships between brands and their customers and explain why customers' expectations of a brand are so important. Successful brands must uphold and live up to those customer expectations through the brand experience, marketing, culture, and behavior. Perhaps most importantly, we'll analyze if and how a brand can recover after breaking those expectations and leaving customers disappointed and feeling let down.

Using real-world case studies ripped from the headlines, this book will decode and analyze major branding disasters that became front-page news. We'll discuss what each brand did right and wrong, the effect on the brand, and how they got through it. These real-life case studies will help company leaders and branding professionals understand how to build and protect the foundation of a solid brand through the best and worst of times.

WHY LISTEN TO ME?

I have been doing branding work my entire adult life. I

have a deep passion for the topic. I often tell my clients, "I emerged from the womb branding. I can't not do it."

Branding Is Sex laid out my proven methodology that has helped thousands of companies strengthen their brands and grow exponentially. *Branding Is Sex* also helped me grow and expand. I went from being a respected branding professional to world-renowned expert, thought leader, and sought-after speaker on the topic of botched corporate apologies and major brand screwups. Reporters now have me on speed dial. *USA Today* called me three days in a row in one week to comment on different brand screwups in the news. And boy, there are a lot of them.

Whether you're a CEO, a VP, or a marketing or branding professional, you'll find this book enlightening and useful. The hardest part of writing this book was that major brand screwups keep happening every week, and I can't get them all in. I selected some of my favorites and mixed in branding lessons and strategies that every business leader and marketing professional absolutely needs to know.

So pull on your sweatpants and your bunny slippers, put your feet up, and turn the page. I don't mind if you read this book while peeing...with the bathroom door wide open.

Chapter One

BRANDS ARE
LIKE PEOPLE

Strange-looking machines filled the room. They beeped and whirred, casting a greenish glow onto the walls. Tubes and wires ran across the floor like the back room at Radio Shack. A two-year-old boy lay dying in a hospital bed in Denver. He was in a coma. The doctors had just told his mother the boy was not likely to pull through. She broke down. Her pain was made even more intense because her father, the child's grandfather, was a thousand miles away on a business trip in Los Angeles.

When the grandfather got the news, he rushed to the airport to catch the first flight to Denver. Arriving at the terminal, the security lines were so long he feared he wasn't going to make his flight. He begged the TSA agents to let him cut to the front of the line, but they refused. He waited in line with everyone else.

Once he made it through security, the grandfather sprinted to the departure gate. But the door was already closed. The flight had finished boarding and was preparing for takeoff. What happened next stunned him.

"Are you Mark Dickinson?"

He turned and saw the gate agent looking at him.

"Yes. I'm Mark Dickinson."

The gate agent opened the door to the jetway and said, "We're holding the plane for you."

As Dickinson walked down the jetway, he saw a man wearing a pilot's uniform waiting for him. The pilot said, "Mr. Dickinson, I'm sorry about your grandson. This plane can't go anywhere without me, and I wasn't going anywhere without you. Now relax. We'll get you there. And again, I'm so sorry."

I first heard this story when a friend of mine was telling me about it. As he relayed the details to me, he failed to mention the name of the airline. I said, "Just curious, was that Southwest Airlines?"

My friend said, "Yes, of course it was." It was almost a foregone conclusion, like we didn't even need to ask. That's because the compassionate treatment of customers fits exactly with Southwest's brand.

Southwest is a company I really admire because they show up with a consistent set of beliefs that I understand and can see on display in their interactions with customers. The values and beliefs of Southwest are very clear. They have branded love and respect in air travel.

I see these values play out in the story about the grandfather rushing to see his dying grandson. I see it in their advertising, branding, and marketing. It's in their customer service. It's in the happy, upbeat, lighthearted attitude of the flight attendants and flight crew. It even comes through in things like free drink coupons. They have a cute little message printed on them about love and happiness.

The company's message is consistent. It radiates through everything they do and all customer touchpoints. If I close my eyes, I imagine the Southwest Airlines brand as a living, breathing human with a big, beating heart who wants to give me a warm, squishy hug. I love that.

BRANDS REALLY ARE LIKE PEOPLE

Brands really are like people. More specifically, the brand-customer relationship is analogous to a romantic relationship between two people. First they meet, they become interested in each other, and there is a courtship. Then they begin to date each other exclusively, and eventually, they fall into a well-worn routine of contentment and comfort and being together. That is, until one of them cheats or screws up in some major way.

The relationship between brands and customers is very similar. When you enter into a relationship with another person, you're looking for someone with whom your core values are aligned, someone with similar foundational beliefs. Part of the process of dating and courtship is figuring out if those values do in fact align. And you can learn a lot about someone's values on just one date.

First dates can be a little awkward. The conversation is usually stilted and superficial. You never discuss anything too deep. But you can still learn a lot about the other person's values and belief system. Does the man offer to pick up the check? Does the woman offer to split the check? Is either person rude or condescending to the wait staff? What does each person order? Are they health-conscious and disciplined, or do they lack willpower and self-control? Does the man hold the door for the woman? Does the woman get angry if the man holds the door for her? All these actions speak volumes about a person's values.

The process of courtship is like peeling back the layers of an onion. You slowly get past the tough outer layers until you reach the juicy core values. This is where you get deep into topics, such as children, family, parenting, money, goals, politics, and religion, to name a few. Slowly, the values and belief system of the other person come into focus, and their actions and behaviors start to make sense.

The way people behave, what they say, what they do, how they act, how they engage with other people—in all of those things, you see evidence of values and beliefs. The same is true of a brand. The values and beliefs of a brand drive their actions. The story of the Southwest pilot who held the plane is consistent with that brand's values. I was not surprised when I heard the story. In contrast, when you see a brand behave in a way that is *not* consistent with their values, it's surprising, even jarring. In many cases, it's disappointing or hurtful.

You have values and beliefs as a brand. Whether you like it or not, they are there. Even if a brand hasn't gone through the process of articulating specifically what those values and beliefs are, they are on display for everyone to see with every interaction they have with your brand. It doesn't matter how much clever marketing, advertising, or branding you're doing; if your brand isn't living, breathing, and acting according to your values and beliefs, your brand is broken.

If you don't care for my dating analogies, think of the brand-customer relationship this way. A brand is like a magnet. Just like magnets only attract certain types of metal, a brand is designed to attract certain types of customers who share beliefs and values similar to those of the people and organization behind the brand.

For example, Duluth Trading Company is a clothing brand that knows exactly who their customers are, and they market directly to them. Their customers are fiercely loyal. I know this because when I'm speaking or doing seminars, I always ask the audience which brands they are irrationally loyal to, and Duluth Trading comes up all the time.

Duluth Trading's marketing features a humorous, down-home, midwestern working-man-style irreverence that perfectly fits the audience. Duluth is a relaxed brand for hard working people. Duluth is sort of like the Prairie Home Companion of clothing retailers. They tap into the inner construction worker in all of us. Their website has slogans like, "You only have one butt, don't freeze it off." Their Fire Hose work pants have the slogan, "Tougher than an angry beaver's brood." And all Duluth products come with their famous No Bull guarantee. Head to DuluthTrading.com and read some of their marketing. You'll see what I mean.

THE EMOTIONAL BANK ACCOUNT

In any good relationship, over time, you want to build up equity in the emotional bank account. This happens when you clearly express your values and beliefs, and then consistently behave in a way that's aligned with those stated values and beliefs. Being in consistent alignment with those values means that in every action, every word, every touchpoint, those values shine through.

Think about the people in your life that you love and cherish. You know them so well they are totally predictable, right? You know what they believe and what they value. You know how they will behave in a given situation. That's one of the reasons you love them—because you can predict how they're going to treat you, you like how they treat you, you admire them, you feel close to them, you feel invested in their success, and you know you can depend on them. You are confident that they have your back and that they won't let you down. As a result, they become an important, indispensable part of your life.

Brands also build loyalty this way. They are clear about what they stand for. They are consistent in their actions.

And eventually, they become meaningful and indispensable to their customers.

SELF-EXPRESSIVE BENEFITS

The best relationships are the ones that elevate a person's self-concept. When I am with the man that I love, I feel like I'm on top of the world. Whatever stupid thing I did or failed to accomplish that day is completely okay. Conversely, whatever achievement I have made feels that much greater when we're together. If I bake cookies or make dinner, he will tell me how delicious they are. He elevates my self-concept. The same is true of a great brand.

Great brands elevate a person's self-concept when they use that brand's products. The best brands in the world are the ones that give people the feeling that they have the world on a string—or life by the balls if you prefer to think of it that way. Great brands say something about the user and make them feel awesome about themselves. Amazing brands make their customers feel like taking a roll in the hay, so to speak.

As I describe in my previous book, *Branding Is Sex*, there are three "brand questions" that must be asked and answered in order to build the foundation of a great brand. These questions are designed to get at the core DNA of a brand. When doing market research, most brands never ask their customers these critical questions. Instead, they ask silly things like, "How did we do? What do you like about us? What don't you like?" When branding professionals ask their customers those trite questions, they miss both the big picture and the important nuances of how their brand shows up in the world.

The first question is, "What does it say about a person that they use this brand?" Does using a particular brand tell the world you're a risk taker, upwardly mobile, and cutting edge? Or does it say you prefer baking Tollhouse cookies, wearing Christmas sweaters, and driving a minivan? The brands we choose speak volumes about us, and we know that.

The functional features and benefits of two similar products from different brands might be exactly the same. But the customer chooses one brand over another because it helps him communicate something not only to the rest of the world but also *to himself about himself* through its use.

Question number two is, "What is the singular thing customers get from this brand that they cannot get anywhere else?" Customers choose great brands because those brands are singular in delivering on a very specific promise for the customer. Great brands are not different just for the sake of being different. In fact, it's not enough just to be different. You have to be *meaningfully* different by being singular. Question number two really gets to the essence of the oneness of your brand; it's the part of the brand that makes you, you. What job is your brand doing for the customer that no other brand can do?

The third question, and the most important one, is, "How does the brand make the customer the hero in their own story?" This question makes all the difference in the world. It's basically asking, how does the brand get customers laid? People choose products that help them tell the story of their life. If you can make your customers feel like the hero in their own movie, you have a customer for life.

When you ask these three questions and really think through the answers, that is the true DNA of your brand. It's the emotional core of your brand. Asking these three questions will help you identify the brand values and beliefs which will then guide all future actions. The clearer you get with your answers to the three questions, the stronger your brand promise will be.

NEVER TAKE YOUR EYE OFF THE BALL

Whether you are building a brand, reigniting a brand, or just checking your brand promise and validating it to make sure that it can withstand whatever trauma could potentially occur, go back and make sure that you can answer those questions in a meaningful way. If you can't, you may have taken your eye off the ball and stopped thinking about the brand. This does happen, especially when companies are growing fast. It's easy to forget about branding and renege on your promise to your customers. You have to think about branding always and often. You can never take a break from branding.

When you let the brand promise languish, that's when customers begin to defect. If you're not talking to your customers constantly, if you're not in touch with their needs, what's important to them, and how their values are changing, you could put your brand in danger of extinction. A brand can go extinct in two ways—through blunt force trauma to the brand (which I'll talk about in this book), or simply dying on the vine by losing touch with its customers and gradually becoming irrelevant.

Now more than ever, branding professionals can never take their eye off the ball. In today's world, we have instantaneous, always-on communication. Branding must also be an always-on activity. If you lose focus, other people can own your brand narrative before you even get a chance to correct the record. Being in touch with, and staying relevant to, your customers has become more of an imperative than ever.

RETIRING THE FOUR P'S

When I was in business school, they taught us about the Four P's of marketing—product, pricing, placement, promotion. The concept being taught was that marketing and branding are a cognitive pursuit; all you had to do was manipulate these four levers (the Four P's) at the right time and in the right way, and people would buy your product. That may have worked once upon a time, but in today's digital/social world, the Four P's look like quaint folklore. Manipulating product, pricing, placement, and promotion might still be a worthwhile academic exercise, but on its own, it's basically useless in the real world.

It's increasingly difficult to get a potential customer's attention, let alone get them to buy, given the proliferation of media, social media, markets, and distribution channels, not to mention information overload. Simply putting a product in front of a potential buyer and expecting them to buy is naïve. To sell products today, brands must build meaningful relationships with their customers by tapping deeply into the emotions in the heart, just as in human relationships.

Walk into any grocery store today, and you will be overwhelmed by choice. For example, the grocery store near me has twenty-seven different types of bread. How am I supposed to choose? Simple: I don't. Instead, I find myself time and again buying Wonder Bread. It's the brand I have a relationship with. I've known and trusted this brand throughout my entire life, because its values and beliefs align with my values and beliefs, and it behaves in a consistent, predictable, and authentic way.

The Four P's are dinosaurs. And so is just about everything you thought you knew about branding; it's no longer relevant. The reason we buy things is they elevate our self-concept. We're all looking for that feeling of self-actualization. The things that we buy, eat, drink, drive, wear, and own are all about helping us get to our own personal nirvana.

BUILD A BRAND TO BE USED, NOT ADMIRED

You should never build a brand just to be admired. Nevertheless, brands do this all the time. The best brands in the world are those that are built to be *used*. Let me explain.

What this means is that you should build a brand not just with flashy, jazzy, creative marketing or whiz-bang features that grab people's attention on the surface. Don't build a brand that's just provocative and evocative through smoke and mirrors. Build a brand with real substance, a brand that can solve significant problems for customers, that has an honest job to do for its buyers. You don't want to create a brand that's "all hat and no cattle." You want a brand with substance. That substance comes from solving problems, elevating a person's self-concept, and helping them be the hero in their life.

I have purchased plenty of products because they seem cool, flashy, and different, and they have a clever marketing pitch. But once I get the product home and actually live with it, I realize it's not materially different or useful in any meaningful way. I was lured in by the sizzle. So what happens? The product sits on a shelf or in a box in the garage and is never used. Or, I return it to the store.

For example, I am the proud owner of dozens of useless kitchen gadgets—slicers and dicers and bladed gizmos of all shapes and sizes. (Remember the Salad Shooter?) In every case, I bought it because I fell for a slick sales pitch that convinced me that this new gadget would make my life in the kitchen easier. But when I actually put these gadgets to use, I gradually realized that they actually create more work for me and that the best slicer and dicer is still the plain old kitchen knife.

You can't build a lasting brand by selling products that no one wants to use. Smart branding professionals know that customers don't buy things just to have them. No one buys a $400 juicer just to look at on their kitchen counter. Smart brands create products that are useful in solving an acknowledged problem. The better the product does at solving that problem, the more loyal customers there will be.

Sometimes, however, the problem that the product solves isn't the obvious or most basic problem. For example, I love Valentino shoes. I have several pairs because I think they're gorgeous and I love wearing them. In a literal sense, the problem shoes as a product category are designed to solve is not having to walk around barefoot. But that's not at all why I buy Valentinos. The reason why women buy a pair of Valentino pumps with five-inch heels and pointy toes and spikes all over them has nothing to do with protecting their feet. It has everything to do with portraying a certain image. When I wear my Valentinos, it projects an image of me as a woman of style who deserves nice things and who has arrived in her life.

People will buy expensive products where the functional benefits are not necessarily obvious because it says something about them as a person. Or it makes them feel a certain way. It's not always for the functional benefit; it's for the emotional benefit.

MAKE THE CUSTOMER THE HERO

Building products that customers want to use is important, but it's only part of the story. Great brands create products that also forge an emotional connection by making the customer the hero in their own story.

Women do not buy designer handbags because they have unique features or are more functional than cheaper bags. Designer bags do the exact same thing as bags that cost a fraction of the price. We buy them because they make us feel like the hero in our own story.

People don't buy a certain brand of running shoes just because they want to use them to run. When it comes down to it, I can probably run just fine in a pair of generic $19 running shoes from Costco. But instead, I buy $130 Hoka One One Clifton 5 running shoes. Are they five times better than cheap running shoes? Maybe, maybe not. But I like what it says about me to other runners on the trail that I run in Hoka One Ones. We buy a certain brand of running shoes because they're part of making us the hero in our own story. That's where that emotional component comes in.

To use the romantic relationship analogy again, women do not choose a mate purely to procreate and avoid lone-liness. If that was all we required, we could find a mate in fifteen minutes. "Penis and a pulse? Yup. Hop in."

That is not the path that we choose in life because we are complex beings with the power of abstract thought. We want a man to stroke the gooey inner part of our hearts. We choose a mate because they're going to add value to our lives, and they're going to help us ascend on the hierarchy of needs to the point that we have reached our nirvana, not because we're just trying to satisfy loneliness or get laid.

Brands really are like people. When Southwest Airlines held that flight so the grandfather could get to his dying grandson in Denver, the airline acted like a person. Humans have compassion, feelings, values, and beliefs. So do great brands.

Chapter Two

———

HOW THE WORLD OF BRANDING IS DIFFERENT TODAY

Just as the world of politics has changed in the era of Donald Trump, so has the world of branding. I recently spoke at the annual convention of the American Association of Political Consultants. It was their big conference where both Democrats and Republicans gather to discuss strategy. They invited me to give the keynote. I also attended some of the breakout sessions and the parties. Democrats and Republicans drinking and partying together, who knew?

I titled my presentation, "What the Actual F**k, Trump's 2016 Master Class in Strategic Branding."

I'm not a Donald Trump supporter by any means. I don't agree with his message. At all. But from a branding standpoint, his 2016 presidential campaign was sheer brilliance. Donald Trump's campaign was a master class in the power of branding. As a result, I told the audience that I believe the world of political campaigns is going to change forever in the Age of Trump. Campaigning for political office, particularly for president, will never be the same. In fact, the 2016 Trump campaign has completely changed the way companies, organizations, and individuals show up with their brands.

BT AND AT

BT stands for Before Trump. AT stands for After Trump. In my mind, these are two distinctly different ages of branding, all thanks to the president.

Trump ran a counterintuitive campaign, one that didn't look like any other political campaign in history. It wasn't just different, it was meaningfully different and hit a nerve with millions of voters. Donald Trump was able to master both meaningful differentiation and relevance in his pitch. Differentiation plus relevance equals a brand's power.

His campaign had five key pillars with which he branded himself. First, he was not a politician. He was the *uncandidate,* the dark horse, the outsider, the under-dog who no one expected to mount a serious bid for the presidency.

Second, he did not tailor his message to the typical, politically active voter. Instead, he focused on the people who felt they had been left behind—voters who were disenfranchised, who felt they never had a presidential candidate who stood up for them and cared about their issues. These were predominately white, middle-class men from Middle America—what some people on the coasts call "the flyover states."

Third, he vowed to drain the swamp of Washington. He was going there to shake things up. To turn that town on its head. He knew that tens of millions of voters did not trust the entrenched political class that runs Washington, and he promised to be the new sheriff in town; he put the swamp creatures on notice.

Fourth, Trump built a campaign that relied heavily on nostalgia, recalling a past time when America was at its best and strongest. His ubiquitous slogan, "Make America great again," is both optimistic and reactionary. It implies that great things lie ahead but also that America's past presidents had steered the country down the wrong road and that only Trump could fix it. The promise was that Trump would restore America to its past glory and, in the process, elevate the disenfranchised, forgotten men and women of the heartland.

The fifth thing he did was a cornerstone of his campaign; he was willing to say out loud what people were thinking. No president had ever done that. Past presidents spoke in politically correct, measured, and highly sanitized and guarded speech that was designed to prevent them from being boxed into one position. Trump threw that out entirely. He used brash language, offended everyone under the sun, and spoke his mind without regard for political correctness. This appealed tremendously to voters in Middle America who speak the same way, and value politicians who do.

In stark contrast, Hillary Clinton showed up as experienced and proficient but totally undifferentiated. No one questioned that she had the experience and the skill to lead, but there was no meaningful differentiation between her and every other political candidate in Washington. In short, she looked like just another politician.

Trump completely differentiated himself, even disassociated himself from the entire category (politicians). He was the un-candidate in every way. He financed his own campaign, flew his own private jet, held massive political rallies, and spoke unlike any other politician in history. The way he spoke his mind without a filter offended many people and undoubtedly turned off millions of voters, but it also sucked up all the oxygen in the room and helped Trump dominate the news cycle during the entire campaign. Trump played the outlaw candidate. American voters had never seen this before.

Trump also targeted his message with laser precision on certain issues that appealed emotionally to his ideal customers—working class Americans in red states. Using microtargeting and micromessaging, he spoke to their hearts and appealed to the *emotional core* of each voter. In contrast, Hillary was polished, rehearsed, and focus-group-tested.

Clinton ran a product marketing exercise in which most of her communication was about features and benefits of detailed policy proposals. Her message appealed to the head, not the heart. As a result, she never formed an emotional connection with millions of independent voters. When head competes with heart, heart wins every time.

The lesson from the Trump campaign that I shared in my keynote to the political consultant convention was simple. In the Era of Trump, political candidates must treat their campaign as a *branding* exercise, not a *product marketing* exercise.

TRUMP CHANGED BRANDING FOR EVERYONE

After Donald Trump won the presidency, he assembled a business advisory board made up of CEOs from top US companies. Many were eager to serve and advise the president on creating jobs and growing the economy. That is, until the Charlottesville Unite the Right Rally and Trump's controversial response.

On August 12, 2017, a group of activists gathered in Charlottesville, Virginia, to protest against a white supremacist rally being held the same day. A twenty-year-old man plowed his car into the crowd of protesters, killing a thirty-two-year-old woman named Heather Heyer.

In remarks following the incident, President Trump implied that the activist counter-protesters were partly responsible for the violence. He said, "I think there is blame on both sides. You had a group on one side that was bad and you had a group on the other side that was also very violent. Nobody wants to say it, but I will say it right now."

The country erupted. Trump's critics accused him of defending white supremacists.

In the days following these events, several high-profile CEOs announced they were quitting the presidential advisory board because of the president's comments. CEOs from Pepsi, 3M, Campbell's Soup, J.P. Morgan, GE, and Merck all rejected the president's actions. Trump had no choice but to fold the advisory boards.

From a branding perspective, this was the first time we saw major global brands take a very public stand against a politician in order to reaffirm their beliefs and values. This was the start of a massive change in corporate branding strategy. Since Charlottesville, and repeatedly with a long list of Trump's controversial policies and statements, more and more brands have begun pushing their values and beliefs to the forefront, and leaning in to political debates that were once considered taboo for brands.

President Trump and his policies are highly divisive. The nation is split on many of the controversial issues and executive orders that emanate from the White House. As a result, there is a polarizing effect that almost requires brands to either align themselves with Trump or embrace the resistance movement. It's almost like customers are asking brands to pick a side, "Well, that company took a stand, what's your stand?" Companies need to accept that their values and beliefs are going to be on display and judged, depending on how they act—or don't act—on important issues.

WHAT DO YOU STAND FOR?

Today, customers are accustomed to seeing brands taking

a stand. They *expect* brands to take a stand. For example, on February 14, 2018, after seventeen people died in a mass shooting at Marjory Stoneman Douglas High School in Parkland, Florida, antigun activists demanded action. A dozen major brands responded right away. Bank of America issued a statement saying it would not lend money to companies that make assault-style weapons. Citigroup announced a policy that it would require clients to restrict firearm sales to people age twenty-one and older. Kroger said it would stop selling magazines that feature assault-style weapons. YouTube began banning videos that provided information on how to make guns and gun accessories. LL Bean, REI, Walmart, Dick's Sporting Goods, Publix, and other companies announced similar antigun measures.

Customers are now looking for brands to do the right thing and publicly live up to their values and take a stand either for or against issues. This has become the new normal in branding. When brands don't live up to customer expectations, those customers will criticize the brand on Twitter and even start #BoycottYourBrand campaigns.

It doesn't matter how much you spend on marketing campaigns, branding, and buying media, at the end of the day, one consumer with a single tweet or a video of your brand not behaving in accordance with your stated—or unstated but expected—promise can have serious consequences. There are some brands that can endure that type of crisis, and there are some that can't.

NIKE TAKES A STAND

When NFL quarterback Colin Kaepernick knelt in protest during the National Anthem, he sparked a national controversy. He said he was kneeling to protest racial injustice, a cause that many people support. But in so doing, he alienated half the country. Many sports journalists and commentators worried that Kaepernick had alienated millions of football fans. Conservative cable news pundits called it an outrage, and they predicted Kaepernick would never work again. They were correct—in the NFL at least.

In 2018, when it looked like Kaepernick's career was over, one of the most prestigious brands in the world signed him as the face of their new global ad campaign. Nike had been looking for a star athlete to feature in its ad campaign to commemorate the thirtieth anniversary of the "Just Do It" slogan. They chose Kaepernick.

Wait, what?

Yes, of all the professional athletes in the world, Nike chose Kaepernick. The man who flamed out of the NFL by kneeling during the National Anthem. The man who millions of NFL fans considered to be a disgrace to the game and to the country. The man whom angry NFL fans vilified and condemned on social media. Kaepernick was *persona non grata* both in the NFL and in the living rooms of millions of football fans.

"What was Nike thinking? How stupid is Nike?" I heard people criticize Nike again and again over this. "Nike's sales are going to tank. They made a massive mistake by pissing off NFL fans. Nike is over. The stock price is going to fall."

Actually, the opposite happened.

I knew immediately that signing Kaepernick was a genius branding move. In the face of heated debate and national controversy over Kaepernick's protest, Nike pulled on their big-boy pants and took a stand on a very sensitive and divisive issue—kneeling during the National Anthem. Nike's marketing team knew that a large swath of the country despised Kaepernick. But they also knew that an equally large portion of the population admired him and appreciated his message of equality.

Signing Kaepernick was genius because Nike knows who their core customers are—and who they are not. Their core customers are *not* the stereotypical NFL fans—white, lower- and middle-class men in their forties and fifties who fill football stadiums and chug beer every Sunday. Those guys buy maybe one pair of Nikes every five years and wear them to mow the lawn. Frankly, Nike doesn't care about their values and beliefs. They are not core customers for the brand, so Nike didn't worry about alienating them with Kaepernick.

By signing Kaepernick, Nike showed up with a set of values and beliefs that aligned with the customers who are most predictive of their financial success. The ideal customers Nike wants to please are young people, age eighteen to twenty-five, who fully buy into the Nike brand. Nike stands for tapping into that athlete inside all of us and encouraging young, physically active adults to have an inner dialogue with themselves about what they are willing to do athletically, and how far they are willing to push themselves physically, and now mentally and socially.

In an interview with CNBC, NYU Stern School of Business professor, Scott Galloway, called the Colin Kaepernick decision "the gangster genius brand move of 2018."

BRAND IDENTITY VS. BRAND IMAGE

A brand is a construct made of two parts: brand identity and brand image. Brand identity is the part that you (the brand) owns. Brand image, on the other hand, is the part your customers own.

For most of the past twenty-five years I've been doing branding, companies put way more emphasis on brand identity, which includes the brand strategy process, brand creation, and brand management. In recent years, that emphasis has shifted dramatically toward an equal focus on brand image, which includes what everybody else in the world thinks of your brand. Brand image is based on not just what people experience in using a brand but also the impact of what people see online, in the news, in reviews, on social media, in apps, and on video. Brand image can surge or plummet based on a single video clip, a tweet from a social media influencer, or any communication that drives public opinion.

Brands have to worry about external drivers now more than ever before. This has completely changed the way brands operate.

THE DIGITAL REVOLUTION ENGULFS BRANDING

Snapchat barely existed when I wrote my last book. A few years later, Snapchat is already looking passé. The cool kids don't even use Snapchat anymore. Don't believe me? Take a look at the stock price. As of this writing, Snapchat has lost three-quarters of its value since the IPO. We are living in a post-Snapchat world.

What will the next Snapchat look like? What company will be the next Facebook? No one knows. That's the thing about disruptors: they come out of nowhere. You cannot prepare for the next big communication channel because no one knows what that will be. Your strongest defense—your *only* defense—is to strengthen your brand so you can survive any disruption. You have to build a brand that will endure.

Coca-Cola is so strong it can endure anything, a legacy brand that has always stood for inspiring moments of happiness and connection. Customers have deep ties to the brand, and they trust it. The Coca-Cola brand was built strong from the start, and it's going to endure. Coke can withstand our instantaneous news cycle and always-on communication. Coke will be a strong brand long after Snapchat has come and gone, and long after the next big social media platform has come and gone.

If I were writing this book ten years ago, we would only be talking about branding on the internet. But today, we're talking about creating brands that exist in 360 degrees. We have children and young adults who have grown up as digital natives. They only know a connected world. Everything from instant sports scores to pizza delivery to chauffeured transportation to a date for Netflix-and-chill is just a few screen taps away. We are digitally connected in virtually every aspect of life.

News cycles today are literally instantaneous. The minute something major happens, it hits the digital airwaves and spreads across the country and around the globe. Brands don't get the opportunity to control the narrative anymore. Now more than ever, customers control the narrative, and brands have to react and hope for the best.

With today's always-on social media channels and instantaneous news cycle, when something happens involving your brand, the horse has probably already left the barn long before you have any idea. Millions of people could be reading about your brand crisis before your CEO gets his morning coffee.

So what can a brand do proactively to prevent a branding crisis from spiraling into a disaster? First, make sure everyone in your organization understands your values, beliefs, and your promises to customers. Every single person in the organization must understand how they can deliver on that promise without hesitation. Inevitably, something bad *will* happen, so you'd better build a brand that has a strong enough foundation to withstand a crisis. You must create a brand that will endure, not just in good times but in bad times, because the bad times are going to come, eventually.

GEN X, GEN Z, AND MILLENNIALS

In any branding discussion, it's worth noting that different generations of consumers have different expectations of brands. Each of the major demographic groups is distinct and has its own generational differences that dictate how brands reach them and how they respond. Here is a summary of each group.

Generation X (or Gen X) are the children of the Baby Boomers. They are sandwiched between the Boomers before them and the Millennials who come after them. From a population standpoint, Gen X is one of the smaller groups. Members of this generation have birthdates from the early to mid-1960s all the way to the early 1980s. Gen X is known for entrepreneurship, independence, working hard but seeking a work-life balance, and being skeptical of authority.

Millennials, the generation after Gen X, are also sometimes called Gen Y. Members of this generation have birthdates roughly from the 1980s to early 2000s. Millennials are known for adopting new forms of communication, like social media platforms, digital media, apps, and other mobile technologies. Millennials tend not to be loyal to the brands their parents held in high esteem. Large corporate brands are often not their first choice. They tend to like highly personalized, bespoke brands, handcrafted, on-demand products, and shared economy services (like ride sharing, home sharing, and those annoying dockless scooters littered over the streets and sidewalks of nearly every major city). Millennials have much higher expectations of brands, and they want to know more about the values of the organization behind the product.

Generation Z, well, that's a whole different ball game. Gen Z kids have birthdates beginning in the 2000s and continuing on to the present day. They are the first truly digital generation. By the time they showed up, the internet and the digital economy were already dominating everyday life. One of the first things they saw as newborn babies was probably their father taking a picture of them with his cell phone. They also were children during the Great Recession. They watched their parents get laid off from jobs and the family homes be foreclosed upon. They have an innate distrust of corporate America (remember the "Occupy Wall Street" movement?). They are cause-oriented; they are all about jumping on the bandwagon for social or political causes. They wear their values on their sleeves like logos, and they want brands to take a stand and show up with their own authentic set of values. Their favorite social media platform is YouTube. They are the first generation to question the value of having a college degree. The traditional rites of passage are falling to the wayside with Gen Z. They have different expectations of everything in the world, and that includes brands. People in Gen Z are starting to come into their own in terms of being purchase influencers. As they get older, enter the workforce, and raise families...it will be interesting to watch.

Chapter Three

BRAND-NEW WORLD

The dramatic fall of Hollywood megaproducer Harvey Weinstein sent shockwaves not only through Tinsel Town but through corporate headquarters across the country. Multiple women came forward and made allegations of sexual assault against Weinstein, which led to criminal charges. Weinstein had to step down from his entertainment company, the Weinstein Company, and hire a criminal defense attorney. All of a sudden, one of the biggest big shots in Hollywood was a pariah. The Me Too movement had taken down a movie mogul and destroyed a prolific entertainment brand in a matter of a few weeks.

At first, some of Weinstein's powerful friends tried to stick up for him. Fashion maven Donna Karan expressed public support for Weinstein. Big mistake. Karan and her brand, DKNY, suffered the wrath of angry women and men all over the country for not supporting the alleged victims of sexual assault.

Meryl Streep also saw her reputation tarnished by the Weinstein scandal. Internet memes started popping up, showing Streep hugging and praising Weinstein at awards shows. People began to question whether she knew about Weinstein's actions, and if so, was she complicit?

The allegations against Weinstein are that he preyed on and hurt other human beings for his own gratification. This destroyed not only his career but also his company, and harmed the reputation of anyone who supported him or was associated with him.

The backlash was so fervent it changed the branding land-scape. Brands learned that they have to be responsible not just for their own actions, they must also monitor the actions of the company they keep and those whom they associate and do business with. In the era of the Me Too movement, brands do not operate in a vacuum of one-to-one relationships with their customers. It's not just you. It's your entire ecosystem.

The Weinstein scandal not only destroyed his reputation and The Weinstein Company, but it also hurt the Hollywood brand overall. Hollywood is famous for making movie magic and bringing dreams to life. But for the first time in vivid, disturbing detail, the world got a glimpse of what really goes on in Hollywood, including the long-rumored casting couch and how powerful producers prey on vulnerable people desperate for fame. Now, perhaps for the first time, the public has to worry if buying a movie ticket is, in a way, supporting such reprehensible behavior.

Me Too is just one example of how the whole world in which brands operate is completely different than anything we've ever seen before. There are new sensitivities, there are new ways to purchase things, there are big online companies that are blending the lines between physical and online retail. There are companies blending the lines between social media and consumerism, and there are new ways to market, shop, and purchase goods we haven't even seen yet. This means that brands need to be vigilant about creating the emotional connections that transcend politics (or your company's CEO deciding to, or feeling like she's forced to, get into the political mix), social changes, and the addition and deletion of marketing and sales channels. Brands need to be thoughtful and deliberate about building brand relationships, which requires them to get to the gooey emotional core and focus not on the four P's of marketing alone but on building a brand that can withstand all this tumult.

When my first book came out in 2016, it was totally okay to call myself a brand dominatrix. It was totally okay to have the words 'sex' and 'laid' in the title. But in the era of the Me Too movement, it's no longer acceptable. All of a sudden, a brand message that was fine two years ago is no longer appropriate. The world is rapidly changing, and slogans, brands, and even logos that were clever or funny a couple of years ago are now borderline offensive. Brands have to react to this. Today, society is highly sensitized to issues and causes that didn't even register a few years ago.

The Me Too movement is emblematic of why this book is topical and timely. Major upheavals in society, business, markets, and media are reshaping the branding landscape. Branding is now more important than ever. And avoiding brand disasters is more difficult than ever. In this chapter, we'll examine three of the factors that make branding more critical than ever—the Amazonification of markets, the proliferation of markets and media, and the rise of the activist CEO.

THE AMAZONIFICATION OF MARKETS

I recently made two major additions to my life—a second dog and a lake house. On weekends, I need to transport all my stuff and my two dogs to the lake, so I decided to upgrade my SUV to a larger model with an additional row of seats and more cargo space. When I began looking around at available models, I was stunned.

BRANDING IS ABOUT EMOTION

When we hear about a powerful movie mogul accused of coercing and forcing vulnerable women into sexual acts, we feel certain emotions. We are emotional beings. Humans don't make decisions based only on logic, data, or mathematical calculations. We make decisions with our emotions. Our brains are wired that way.

There are three key parts of the human brain. The frontal and neocortex are where our powers of rational decision-making reside. These include language processing, doing math, and making cognitive decisions.

The area in the brain stem and medulla is the reptilian brain, which is responsible for the fight-or-flight instinct. Can I fight this saber-toothed tiger, or should I run away? Can I trust this person? Is it safe to get out of my car and pump gas at midnight at this sketchy gas station? Can I trust this brand?

Deep in the gooey core of our brain is the limbic system. This is the part of the brain that helps us feel emotion. A famous neuroscientist named Antonio Damasio studied people whose limbic system was no longer functioning so that they lacked the ability to feel emotion. What he found was that people who lacked the ability to feel could not make even basic decisions. He concluded what we all know to be true: we rely on our emotions to make decisions. This indicates there is a connection between brain science and branding.

Every interaction that you have with a person, place, or object throughout the course of your life becomes somehow engrained into your subconscious, helping you make decisions. Humans don't make decisions in a vacuum. We make decisions based on the sum total of all of our life experiences. The ones we know about and the ones that are programmed into our subconscious. We can't deny the fact that we are emotional beings. That's why branding is so powerful and so important.

The amount of competition in the SUV marketplace is astounding. There are no fewer than a dozen manufacturers and more than thirty models to choose from. When you add trim packages, custom options, and paint color, there are literally thousands of different possibilities. How am I supposed to make a decision?

The number of choices is paralyzing. From a branding perspective, what struck me is the sheer volume of competition. This is true not just in automobiles, of course. Take a look around your local grocery store and pay attention to the volume of different choices and the intense competition among companies. Every nook and cranny is stuffed with product. Nowhere is this more obvious than on Amazon.com. Go to Amazon.com and type in "iPhone cover." You'll see a list of thirty items per page and four hundred pages! Amazon sells some of the phone covers directly, but there are also dozens of other independent companies selling on the Amazon website.

Amazon has caused a seismic shift in retailing and in branding. Not that long ago, when I needed a new outfit, a new computer, or a television, I would hop in my car and drive to the local shopping mall. Today, the vast majority of people first go to the internet to begin shopping. If they find what they want, they buy it online without ever stepping foot in a physical store. Often, the very first stop is Amazon.com.

Amazon has become a vast marketplace for thousands—if not millions—of sellers to market their wares to online buyers. Amazon is still like the Wild Wild west. They control all the rules, and your retail or product brand stands to suffer. To shoppers, Amazon is the brand. Whether it's a product sold directly by Amazon, through the fulfilled-by-Amazon process, or by an independent company, Amazon sets the rules. Sometimes, they even set the pricing. They tell sellers the exact price they must charge for their product. This can turn certain categories into a commodity because the availability of similar products has been increased. When that happens, smaller resellers have to bow to pricing pressure.

With Amazon's purchase of Whole Foods, they now have physical store locations that can provide the benefits that only in-person shopping can. With every shopper, they are gathering data about the consumer products people buy. That data can drive Amazon to manipulate their own pricing on their Amazon Basics and Whole Foods 365 brand products to the extent that competing consumer brands will have to change their pricing models. Amazon is not the 800-pound gorilla of retail, it's the 8,000-pound gorilla.

The impact of Amazon is far-reaching. It means brands that want to reach customers independent of Amazon have to build a brand that transcends the selling platform of Amazon. Toys "R" Us is a brand that basically went out of business because of Amazon. After Toys "R" Us folded, Walmart and Target began to sell more toys online. The toy industry is no longer as fun as it used to be. Toys "R" Us used to serve as a testing or proving ground for new toys and games. Mass retailers like Walmart and Target aren't in it for risk, they're going to emphasize selling the products they *know* will sell in volume.

We can call this the Amazonification of markets. With Amazon and other online sales channels, the barriers to entry have been removed. Now anyone with a phone can call up a product broker in China, drop-ship a crate of product to Amazon, and be in business within a month. Even if a product doesn't exist yet, an entrepreneur can start a KickStarter page based on a diagram, raise money, and start taking orders before a single product rolls off the manufacturing line. This has led to mass competition in just about every space and market.

Along with lowering barriers to entry comes the ease with which companies can be put out of business. There are countless brands that launch with an amazing product that immediately catches on, only to disappear a short time later. Remember Pokemon Go? For an entire summer, you could see people wandering around the sidewalks holding their phone at odd angles playing the game. People were obsessed with Pokemon Go. For a few months, that's all they talked about. But I haven't heard a word about it since. Some other mobile game or app became all the rage, and Pokemon Go was soon a thing of the past.

Every market for every product is competitive. There is a paralyzing amount of choice in practically every market. Four hundred pages of iPhone covers? That makes it really hard for a brand to stand out among all that noise. Anyone can build a business by finding potential customers and then converting them on the basis of price, features, and availability. But in order to build a sustainable, long-lasting brand with repeat customers, one key requirement remains true: you have to build a brand by connecting emotionally with your customers.

THE PROLIFERATION OF MARKETS AND MEDIA

For brands, the good news is the proliferation of markets and media. Today, there are more ways than ever before to reach potential customers. You can sell your stuff on dozens of different platforms, in addition to the traditional channels.

Just a few years ago, everyone was saying, "Too bad you can't sell products on Instagram. Oh, well." But now you can. There is Shoppable Instagram. Soon, we'll have Shoppable Snapchat. My daughter is a college student, and she has friends on campus who are microinfluencers.

Fashion retailers send them free clothes to wear as long as they post about them on Instagram. We're not talking Kardashians here. Their sphere of influence is just a few hundred people. But that's really important to retailers. Who knew five years ago that there would be an entire microinfluencer economy available to brands?

As brands, we have to pay attention to the fact that there are unlimited possibilities and avenues for selling products today. Therefore, we need to create a brand that is consistent and stable, and can endure regardless of what medium you show up in.

RISE OF THE ACTIVIST CEO

In 2018, *Harvard Business Review* published an article titled "The New CEO Activists." The first line of the article states how the phenomenon of CEO activism has grown. "The White House's withdrawal from the Paris climate accord, response to the clash between white supremacists and counter-protesters in Charlottesville, Virginia, and decision to rescind Deferred Action for Childhood Arrivals have galvanized many U.S. corporate leaders to speak out and take action."

CEO activism has thrown companies into politics in a way we haven't seen before. It's become a common occurrence to see CEOs of top companies coming out publicly either for or against some political topic or social justice issue, like the Me Too movement. CEO activism has become the new normal. A survey by the public relations firm Weber Shandwick of more than one thousand Americans found that nearly half of respondents believe CEO activism can make an impact and can even influence government policy.

Increasingly, CEOs feel they have a responsibility to use their power and their megaphone to correct social wrongs and stand up to injustice. The first paragraph of the Weber Shandwick study states, "This year's report finds that nearly eight in 10 consumers (77 percent) agree that CEOs need to speak out when their company's values are violated or threatened."

Since customers are expecting the leaders of the organizations and brands that they patronize to have a point of view on political issues, branding is even more important. When you are the leader of an organization and you take a stand for or against something, that's a stand not just for you as an individual but also for the brand that you represent. You had better be certain that you are very clear on your brand promise and what values your brand stands for before your loudmouth CEO goes out there and starts talking about it. The CEO is often the living logo of a brand, so if they say something outrageous or offensive, the brand suffers.

Your brand isn't just your product or service. The way the public sees things, your brand is made up of every single person who speaks on behalf of your company, including and especially the CEO.

People have higher expectations of brands. Now, brands must have a heightened awareness of everything the brand does, and not just with customers. The stakes are higher than ever to get it right, and it's easier than ever for a brand to screw up bad and have it go all over the world.

The relationship is no longer just between the brand and their customer. Getting back to our relationship analogy, no longer is the relationship just between you and your partner. That relationship now includes your partner's friends, coworkers, parents, siblings, and her drunk uncle Bob. To some extent, what these people do, what they say, how they act, how they behave, even the obnoxious date that your cousin brought to the wedding, it all reflects on *you*. The relationship is not just you and your partner, it's a whole ecosystem.

As the Harvey Weinstein example illustrates, brands need to be concerned about whom they're doing business with, whom they're associating with, and what orbits they're revolving around. All of these things can influence how you're perceived by customers and the world, and can have a far-reaching impact on a brand. The best defense is to build a brand with a strong foundation and be very clear on what your values and beliefs are so that you can deliver consistently on that promise.

Chapter Four

CRISIS OF LEADERSHIP

In the summer of 2017, I witnessed two raging dumpster fires. The first one was burning in an actual dumpster in a deserted back alley of a city in Texas, likely set by some teenage vandals bent on causing mischief. I'm sure the local fire department eventually got around to extinguishing it.

The second raging dumpster fire engulfed the $62 billion valuation mega-startup Uber. And it smelled way, way worse than any actual dumpster fire.

BRO CULTURE

A string of unfortunate and mismanaged events plunged Uber into what seemed like an abyss of unprincipled, exploitative, and shameless actions that threated to destroy the company's reputation. First, there were allegations that CEO Travis Kalanick and top management ran the company like a fraternity, fostering a "bro culture," and subsequently ignoring a number of sexual harassment and discrimination complaints from employees. Second, the company was accused of using aggressive and unfair competition strategies, like trying to take out competitors in their marketplaces. Third, the company failed to acknowledge a massive cyberattack that exposed millions of their customers' personal data, a revelation followed by allegations that the company then tried to cover up the scandal.

The combination of these events brutalized Uber's reputation and turned off millions of customers. In fact, some frustrated Uber riders and drivers created the #DeleteUber movement in an attempt to punish the company for its perceived transgressions. The unflattering #DeleteUber hashtag circulated wildly across social media and caused grave concern in the Uber executive suite.

In June 2017, Uber founder, Kalanick, announced he was taking a leave of absence. He said he wasn't stepping down as CEO, he was just out of his role for a while. Uber's board then decided to bring in former US Attorney General, under President Obama, Eric Holder, to conduct a comprehensive investigation into the company's culture.

Holder's findings were stunning. A toxic culture and rampant bad behavior in the company emanated from the top down. Unfair treatment of employees, sexual harassment, and discrimination were found to be not only pervasive but actually encouraged and even rewarded in some cases. Critics accused Kalanick of creating a bro culture in the executive suite and then driving it down through the rest of the organization.

Shortly after the Holder findings, Kalanick, a Silicon Valley darling and multibillionaire founder of one of the most successful startups in the world, stepped down as CEO. Former Microsoft executive, Dara Khosrowshahi, took over as CEO and was immediately tasked with restoring the company's reputation and trust with customers.

CRISIS OF LEADERSHIP

Founder-led startups tend to take on the culture of their leaders. When a company has a bigger-than-life founder and CEO who behaves in a certain way, it doesn't matter what the brand promotes in its marketing materials or its advertising because the CEO is setting the tone and the direction of the organization. On the positive side, founder-led cultures can be very strong because they're driven by the passion and vision of the founder, and that can inspire employees. Employees tend to rally around a charismatic founder.

But the downside risk is that a founder/CEO can lead a company into a toxic culture. That founder is often seen by the employees as the ultimate embodiment of the company's brand in human form. As the founder/CEO goes, so goes the company. In Uber's case, a crisis of leadership at the top took the company down the wrong path.

I know many people reading this book are either founders and CEOs, or you aspire to be. Whether you are the CEO or will be one day, beware. Heed the warnings in this chapter. Your passion, your energy, and your love for the company as a founder are part and parcel to your brand. That's a great thing. But if you screw up, if you behave badly, if you behave in a way that betrays your brand promise, you really can bring down the whole company.

Uber is a cautionary tale. Years after their raging dumpster fire, the company under CEO Khosrowshahi is still trying to repair the brand and reestablish the brand promise and rebuild customer trust.

WHEN CEOS GO WILD

As I wrote in a 2018 article for TheDrum.com about chief executives going wild, "Our history books are full of stories of powerful, tyrannical leaders taking advantage of their subjects. The past few years have revealed corporate execs engaging in insider trading, expressing unpopular and controversial beliefs, committing every variety of fraud and being outright bigots and assholes. More recently, we've seen what seems like an endless parade of corporate leaders sexually discriminating [against] and harassing people in their workplaces or being complicit when other employees have done so. I'm fairly certain that none of these are new phenomena."

But what is new is the speed at which these bad behaviors travel and gain public notoriety. When a CEO behaves badly, even in private, the world will soon find out.

SAY BYE TO PAPA

In late 2017, Papa John's CEO, John Schnatter, blamed the NFL player protests during the National Anthem for declining sales at Papa John's. To make matters worse—much worse—a few months later, Schnatter admitted to using a racial slur during a conference call. Critics and civil rights groups called Schnatter a bigot and a racist.

The criticism that ensued engulfed the company and had a material effect on its financial performance. Sales plunged by double digits, and the stock plummeted to a five-year low. Many of the operators of Papa John's locations feared they could lose their stores. Schnatter resigned as CEO.

When brands put their corporate leaders on display as

the face of their brand, they're at especially high risk for a branding disaster. Often, these disasters are due to a crisis of leadership. Papa John's built its success on the story of John Schnatter—the everyday guy who started making pizzas by hand, bootstrapped the company expansion, and grew it into a massive organization. Schnatter's first name is part of the name of the company. He literally *is* Papa John. His picture is on the wall in every store. He's featured in every commercial. He is the company spokesperson, and he's the living logo of the brand.

Schnatter reacted to the racial epithet controversy in precisely the wrong way. He didn't take responsibility until it was too late. He blamed other people. He got into a very public disagreement with the leadership of his own company. He adopted the attitude that the brand doesn't exist without him. All around awful behavior that tarnished Papa John's.

TROUBLE AT CBS

Les Moonves's name wasn't tied to his company the way John Schnatter's was, but as CEO of CBS, he was a highly visible leader. He's another example of when the leader at the top acts in a way that isn't in accordance with what the expectations are for the brand, how it can put a black mark on the entire company.

Moonves was a vocal advocate of the Me Too movement. He is a founding member of an organization called the Commission on Sexual Harassment and Advancing Equality in the Workplace. But in July 2018, six women accused Moonves of sexual harassment, intimidation, and abuse. The CBS board investigated.

Then the *New Yorker* reported that six additional women had come forward with allegations dating back decades. There was even an unsubstantiated allegation that CBS had a woman on staff for the sole purpose of providing oral sex to Mr. Moonves upon demand. Wow. I can't even get my mind around how sick and twisted that is. CBS? Really? I really hope that is not true.

Moonves resigned as CEO on September 9, 2018. Due to the allegations, his alma mater, Bucknell University, removed Moonves from its website, as did the University of Southern California.

Moonves denied the allegations. In a statement to *Variety* he wrote, "Untrue allegations from decades ago are now being made against me that are not consistent with who I am."

The Moonves scandal is particularly poignant because he was the head of an entertainment company that piped its product into the living rooms of almost every home in America. Moonves had a hand in some of the top television programming ever created. *The Big Bang Theory, NCIS, Survivor, 60 Minutes, CSI, Everybody Loves Raymond.* It didn't compute to consumers that the guy who brought us such family-oriented programming could be the same person who allegedly sexually harassed and abused so many women. This is the part that leaves most people so disappointed. His real, authentic behind-the-scenes behavior didn't match what we thought was his public persona—his brand—which was all about bringing families together in the living room to watch TV. After the allegations broke and Moonves resigned, I'm sure many people looked at CBS programming in a whole new light.

It reminds me of when I was a kid at Disney World and the lights came on inside Space Mountain. I could see all the wires, concrete, and rusty metal. It ruined the fun by revealing the sad reality behind the magic. Innocence lost.

LATER, LAUER

The egregious allegations against NBC's Matt Lauer invoked a similar feeling in me. Lauer was like America's dad. Millions of viewers began their day watching Lauer and his crew yuck it up on NBC's *Today* show. Lauer would laugh and smile, spewing happy talk all over Rockefeller Center. He seemed like a cool, nice, pleasant person that you'd want to be around. He was the human embodiment of the NBC brand.

I was crushed when a lengthy list of allegations publicly accused Lauer of sexual misconduct. I felt duped. If the allegations were true, if he really whipped out his penis in front of a frightened female staffer, this man who seemed so nice was in reality a perverted creep at best or, worse, a sexual predator.

It seemed Lauer was not the man I thought he was, and it brought everything into question for me. My emotional relationship with the *Today* show brand—and to a lesser extent, NBC—came tumbling down. I felt dirty for watching him all those years. I switched to another network for my morning TV.

When the face of an organization is caught behaving badly, it brings the culture of the entire organization into question. One might legitimately wonder, "If the top dog behaves like a literal dog, has he enabled or emboldened other company leaders and managers to act in a similar manner? Is he complicit in that behavior?" I think it's a fair question.

MARIO'S MELTDOWN

Mario Batali is a chef, restauranteur, cookbook author,

entrepreneur, and television personality. He owns or co-owns restaurants around the country, including the popular Eataly market-style restaurants.

In 2017, four women accused Batali of sexual misconduct and harassment. Within days, four more women came forward. The New York Police Department began an investigation. Batali admitted he acted inappropriately, but denied an allegation of sexual assault. In a statement he said, "My past behavior has been deeply inappropriate and I am sincerely remorseful for my actions." Hey, I'll give him some credit. At least he apologized.

An apology wasn't enough.

Batali took a leave of absence from his company. Executives at ABC television network asked him to stop appearing on the daily TV show *The Chew*. They fired him a few days later. Food Network cancelled his upcoming show titled *Molto Mario*. Target stores pulled Batali's products from store shelves, including pasta sauces and cookbooks. Then Batali's company announced it would be closing its three restaurants on the Las Vegas Strip because the Las Vegas Sands Corporation decided to end their relationship with Batali.

Batali's company likely lost millions of dollars due to his alleged behavior.

BEWARE THE FACE OF THE BRAND

There are many benefits to founder-led organizations, like Mario Batali's company. The drive and inspiration of the founder can catapult the company to tremendous success. But you must also accept the downside.

Corporations put themselves at an accelerated level of risk when they have a single human being as the face of their brand. Because when customers see that person behaving in a way that is inconsistent with their ideal of the brand, it brings their entire relationship with the brand into question.

A company leader's public face and image must match the values of the company. When a famous CEO or founder slips up in a public way, not only do they suffer, but the brand suffers as well. As the cases of Uber, Papa John's, Les Moonves, and Mario Batali show us, you can't promote your brand's values and then have them contradicted by the words or actions of the CEO.

PITCHMAN NO MORE

A single nonfounder, non-CEO who is the face of a brand also creates high risk. Consider Subway restaurants. They went all in on their national spokesperson and pitchman, Jared Fogle. He wasn't the CEO, but he certainly was the living logo of the brand. He was the face of Subway and appeared in their advertising campaigns from 2000 to 2015.

Fogle's reign as spokesperson ended when he pleaded guilty to child pornography charges and traveling to pay for sex with minors. He's now serving a fifteen-year sentence in federal prison. I don't think Subway has ever recovered from this.

BRANDING IS EVERYONE'S JOB

Don't make a single human being the logo of your brand. Doing so can jeopardize the entire company. You cannot predict or manage human behavior, especially humans in powerful positions. Brands must be vigilant that their top executives and pitchmen are fully aligned with the brand promise through and through. It's the best defense against a failure of leadership.

Branding is everyone's job. The leader of the organization needs to head up the effort and buy into the brand values fully, whether that person is the public face of the brand or not, and drive the brand values through that organization. Part of a CEO's job is to deliver the brand experience in 360 degrees, at every level of the company.

The head of the organization bears a huge responsibility for living the brand's values. When a leader publicly and spectacularly fails to live up to those values, today more than ever, it becomes front-page news across the country. CEOs must lead by example.

Additionally, the CEO must demand that every single person in the organization is going to be hired, fired, incentivized, measured, compensated, rewarded, and encouraged based on how they uphold the values of the organization and deliver on the promise of the brand. But leaders can't authentically demand that employees do that unless they are also prepared to do it themselves. Otherwise, it's just bullshit, and people can tell it's bullshit.

Chapter Five

CRISIS OF CULTURE

The horror of witnessing a bloody, unconscious man being forcibly removed from an airplane by two burly security thugs is not something anyone will soon forget. So when it happened on a United Airlines flight—and was recorded on digital video by several passengers, of course—the story and the graphic videos went viral.

I remember when it happened—even though I wasn't there—because nearly a dozen people shared the video with me within minutes. The good news is that this infamous incident apparently changed the way airlines treat passengers who are bumped from flights. The bad news is that the passenger who was forcibly removed was left humiliated and bleeding, and the airline suffered one of the worst branding disasters of the year, if not the entire decade.

Corporate culture is the sum total of the behaviors, attitudes, values, and beliefs of everyone inside the organization. If that's out of whack with your expected and stated brand promise, then you have a crisis of culture. United certainly did.

On April 9, 2017, United had overbooked flight number 3411 from Chicago to Louisville. After the passengers had boarded the plane, a flight attendant announced the plane was overbooked and they needed four passengers to give up their seats. The airline offered $400 in vouchers.

Because 3411 was the last flight to Louisville that day, there were no takers. Instead of offering more money, the airline selected four passengers to be bumped involuntarily. Three of the four agreed, and left the plane willingly. But the fourth, Dr. David Dao, a medical doctor from Louisville, said he had to be at the hospital in the morning and refused to leave the plane.

The United gate agent called uniformed security officers to escort Dr. Dao off the plane. He still refused. That's when the horror show began. Three big guys forcibly grabbed Dr. Dao and yanked him out of his seat. Dao screamed bloody murder, and apparently banged his head and became unconscious. They dragged him down the aisle of the airplane, his shirt pulled up, exposing his midsection, while blood ran down his cheeks. It was a horrific sight.

Dozens of passengers recorded the entire incident on their smartphones. Within minutes, they had shared the video on social media, sent it to all their friends, and submitted it to news outlets. Within hours it became the biggest national news story of the week. One video reached nearly twenty million views on Facebook before it was removed.

As the story went viral it caused an immediate backlash against United. Tweets referred to the airline as barbaric and horrific. One Twitter user wrote, "United Airlines turning flights into the Hunger Games. Volunteer as tribute or get dragged out."

Instead of apologizing immediately, United didn't issue a statement until the next day. Here's what it said:

> Flight 3411 from Chicago to Louisville was overbooked. After our team looked for volunteers, one customer refused to leave the aircraft voluntarily and law enforcement was asked to come to the gate. We apologize for the overbook situation. Further details on the removed customer should be directed to authorities.

In other words, "Sorry not sorry." Wow! United kicks the

crap out of a passenger in front of a full cabin of horrified customers, and that's how they respond? I knew this was not going to end well for United.

When the CEO, Oscar Munoz, finally responded, it was way too little and way too late. First, he responded with a tweet. Strike one. Second, he apologized only "for having to re-accommodate (translation: kick off the plane) these customers." Strike two. Third, he didn't apologize for kicking the shit out of one of them and dragging him unconscious, half-naked and bloody off the plane. No mention of that. Strike three.

Well, at least things couldn't get any worse for United at this point. The company couldn't possibly screw this up any more than they did already, right? Umm...wrong.

In an internal letter to United employees—which of course leaked immediately to the media—CEO Munoz actually *blamed the victim!* The letter stated that Dr. Dao refused to get off the aircraft and "became more and more disruptive and belligerent," so United had to bring in their goons. In other words, Dr. Dao deserved the ass-whoopin' he got. CEO Munoz even said that he supported the beatdown that was dished out. He wrote, "I also emphatically stand behind all of you," and, "Our employees followed established procedures."

Really, Oscar?

Within hours of obtaining that letter, the *Huffington Post* ran a front-page story with the headline (in all caps), "UNITED CEO BLAMES THE VICTIM!" By that night, the story was the top trending story in China and other countries around the world. Hashtags like #UnfriendlySkies and #BoycottUnited began trending, and memes of #NewUnitedAirlinesMottos became a fun pastime online. When the stock market opened the following day, United's share price plunged. The company lost $350 million dollars in market value in a single day.

That share price drop apparently woke up Oscar Munoz. He finally issued a proper statement: "I deeply apologize to the customer forcibly removed and to all the customers aboard. No one should ever be mistreated this way. I want you to know that we take full responsibility and we will work to make it right."

THEY DID EVERYTHING WRONG

United did everything wrong. United's public relations team is made up of really smart people. Their CEO is a brilliant guy. He was once recognized with a Communicator of the Year award. But they still screwed this up royally. And they paid dearly for it.

The first thing the airline should have done was issue a sincere apology to everyone affected by what happened, most notably to Dr. Dao. Ideally, the CEO would have immediately called a press conference and issued a personal, heartfelt, on-camera apology. If that was not possible, then a heartfelt written statement, or a video. If I were writing that apology, it would sound something like this.

We are deeply sorry that we injured a passenger, and that we freaked out other passengers who watched it happen. It is our goal to take care of our customers. And we behaved in a way that is completely against everything we believe in. We take full responsibility for what happened here. We are conducting our own investigation. We are cooperating with authorities. We will get back to you within twenty-four hours with more information and a distinct plan for what we're going to do to prevent this from ever happening again.

We value human lives. They are of utmost importance to us. We feel for the people who were impacted by this, specifically Dr. David Dao. There's no excuse for our behavior. There's no excuse for what anybody did. We feel specifically bad about the people who were looking on while this happened. You should never, ever, ever have to go through anything like that. We will do everything in our power to make this situation right for everyone involved. You have our word as an organization that we will show you a plan for ensuring that this never happens again.

Instead of saying that, United's first response was basically, "We're going to look into this and see if we screwed up here or if it was the passenger's fault. We don't know. We'll get back to you whenever we know more."

But by far, the biggest mistake United made was not responding soon enough, and when they did respond, doing it with a tweet. A full forty-eight hours went by before the CEO issued a proper apology. In the meantime, Twitter and Facebook went wild with biting satire and hilarious memes that skewered United. Reporters around the world wrote stories, and every one lambasted United for their silence. I personally did more than a dozen interviews with the press about what happened and United's lack of an appropriate response.

Everyone was talking about United, except United.

LESSONS LEARNED

There are two big lessons here. The first one is that when a crisis happens, if you don't control the narrative, then your audience will. That's exactly what happened here. United left it up to the public to control the conversation about the brand. The narrative quickly became, "United Airlines doesn't just hate their customers. They physically abuse them."

The second lesson is about the importance of having a healthy corporate culture. I would argue that United had a sick culture at the time of this incident. There is no other explanation for it. And culture starts at the top.

This was not just a case of botched crisis management or a misguided public relations strategy. It went deeper than that. The entire culture at the airline was sick. This was a brand with a broken brand promise. Their brand promise is to be the most caring airline in the world. In fact, United plastered that sentiment all over their marketing materials, on their website, and in all their press releases. Ha! That's laughable. And the entire world saw what a sham it was during the David Dao incident.

If you're going to be the most caring airline in the world, then be that. Live up to that brand promise. This means that culturally you need to drive those values through every single role within the company. This goes for not only your direct employees but also for your vendor partners, suppliers, and contractors who come in contact with United employees. You have to drive that brand promise and hold people accountable for delivering on that promise by empowering them, and enabling them to do whatever it takes to live up to that brand promise.

If United Airlines was really the most caring airline in the world—if they gave a shit about customers at all, really—they would be trained on how to deliver on that brand promise through and through. That flight crew would have been authorized to offer $1,000 to bumped passengers, or even $1,500. I know I would agree to be bumped for that.

THE BONUS LOTTERY, REALLY?

United established a bonus program for their employees. The company set aside a certain pot of money to be distributed to full-time staff. In most companies, bonuses are performance-based—a way to incentivize employees to work hard and go the extra mile to serve customers. Bonuses encourage employees to deliver on the brand promise.

But United had a different idea. They set up the bonus program as a lottery. Literally, a game of chance, like a raffle drawing in which a handful of employees were to get the privilege of sharing in a pot of money. The best corporate bonus programs are those that are tied to specific metrics or key performance indicators and encourage and reward employee behaviors that reinforce the organization's core values. The United lottery bonus program, however, was based on variability and unpredictability—the last two things anyone would want in an airline. A bonus program like that runs the risk of sending exactly the wrong message to employees. This flawed bonus system further underscores why I say United had a crisis of culture.

One final note on the United story. After the stock dropped immediately after the Dr. Dao incident, many people I talked to thought United was in big financial trouble. Domestic airlines operate in a world where competition is somewhat limited, and therefore consumer choice is limited. Even if consumers wanted to #BoycottUnited, it would be much more difficult than, say, switching to a different brand of toothpaste. It's a matter of practicality not principle here. Sometimes consumers just don't have a choice to vote with their wallets.

The public has a generally short memory. Most scandals are short-lived, and are soon replaced in the headlines by more recent scandals. A sick corporate culture, however, can last for years. Not surprisingly for United, the hits kept on coming. Just a few weeks after the Dr. Dao debacle, a pet rabbit mysteriously died on a United flight. Less than a year later, a puppy died on a United jet after a flight attendant demanded the dog go in the overhead bin during the flight. In another pet scandal, United mistakenly flew a family's German Shepherd to Japan instead of Kansas. I have a strong feeling that United will be back in the news very soon—and not for anything good.

WELLS FARGO

Wells Fargo is one of the oldest and most conservative banks in America. They remained a strong financial institution during the Great Recession by avoiding risk. But in 2017, customers learned that Wells Fargo was also one of the shadiest banks to do business with.

I have all my accounts with Wells Fargo, including my business accounts. The trouble they got into affected me personally. I followed their screwup closely. The way they handled the situation was misguided, to say the least.

In 2017, thousands of Wells Fargo customers began to notice suspicious activity on their banking statements. Oddly, new bank accounts, new lines of credit, or new credit cards appeared out of the blue. To make matters worse, on the new accounts—which the customers neither asked for nor authorized—the bank charged high fees.

Complaints began to pour in to the company. Wells Fargo eventually admitted that its employees had been opening up additional accounts without their customers' consent. I know this from personal experience because I was one of those account holders. It was perplexing at first, and then infuriating.

After the story became public, the company tried to blame rogue employees who were acting on their own.

It turned out there was pressure from management to open as many new accounts as possible in order to collect more fees. The government fined Wells Fargo $185 million, and the company now faces civil lawsuits and a criminal investigation. Wells Fargo CEO, John Stumpf, resigned over the scandal. Worst of all, the bank's long-standing reputation as a conservative, reliable, stable financial institution crumbled.

In 2018, the story got worse for Wells Fargo. New allegations surfaced that the bank was forcing customers to purchase unneeded and unnecessary insurance policies. Again, so they could charge more fees. These allegations could lead to an additional one billion dollars in fines against the bank, not to mention more lawsuits. This further eroded the trust customers once had in the brand.

Talk about a sick corporate culture. That blatant disregard for ethics can only come from the top down. These are symptoms of a rotten organization.

But the good news is Wells Fargo handled this branding disaster with aplomb, right? Ha! Not even close. They botched it royally.

I expected the new Wells Fargo CEO, Tim Sloan, to go public with a sincere apology, and a promise to clean house and never let such shenanigans happen again. As a customer, I felt I deserved an apology. I expected the CEO to take responsibility. But that's not what they chose to do.

In response to the public relations debacle, Wells Fargo launched an ad campaign. They called the campaign, "Re-Established." They designed the campaign to help Wells Fargo move past the scandal, reassure their customers, and reinforce their long-standing reputation as a stable, trustworthy, conservative financial institution.

The campaign's slogan was, "Wells Fargo, established 1852. Re-established 2018." In the ads, they very briefly alluded to the scandal, but moved past it quickly. No apology. No video of the CEO saying, "We take full responsibility for our actions." You can see these ads on the Wells Fargo YouTube channel.

So what did the ads focus on? That damned stagecoach! The same dusty old stagecoach they're so proud of. Instead of a campaign saying they're sorry for taking advantage of their customers and promising never to do it again, they dusted off the old stagecoach and filmed it driving through the desert. Genius!

The Wells Fargo stagecoach is just window dressing on the brand. That campaign says to me that Wells Fargo is a company where image doesn't match substance. It says the most important thing about Wells Fargo is that it's been around for 150-plus years, since the old Wild West days. "So look at our stagecoach and hopefully that will distract you from the way we abused our customers and betrayed their trust. Yeah, we totally betrayed you and tried to overcharge you, but isn't our stagecoach pretty?" Fail.

This lukewarm and ineffective response to a massive scandal brought the entire Wells Fargo culture into question. It made me think Wells Fargo is not really serious about owning up to their mistakes and working hard to repair the damage they did to their relationship with their customers.

The campaign left major questions unanswered and unaddressed. How did this customer abuse happen? Why did it go on so long? Why didn't the bank apologize and take full responsibility? What kind of company—especially a financial institution—pressures its employees to fraudulently open up fake bank accounts on behalf of its customers...without ever telling the customers? That is the sign of a sick culture.

Wells Fargo clearly had a crisis of culture.

In the last chapter, we talked about company leadership being responsible for the brand: they have to own it, they have to drive it, they have to live it every day, they have to get everyone in the organization to buy in. The same holds true for establishing a healthy corporate culture: it has to come from the top down. Everyone in the company needs to know what the brand promise is, and every single person in the company needs to behave in accordance with that brand promise. When the leaders at the top of an organization lose their way, the rest of the company will follow.

FACEBOOK'S WORST YEAR EVER

In recent years, Facebook has come under intense public and government scrutiny. First, it was demonstrated that Russian operatives used Facebook to plant fake news stories in an attempt to influence elections. Next, politicians criticized Facebook for unethically sharing data with a company called Cambridge Analytica, which attempted to influence the 2016 presidential elections. Then there were reports of Facebook endlessly tweaking algorithms and censoring certain users. On top of all that, Facebook admitted that hackers breached Facebook's security and stole the personal, private data of millions of users.

As a result, Facebook began to fall out of favor with millions of people. The hashtag #DeleteFacebook began trending. Soon the US Congress demanded that Mark Zuckerberg show up and answer for these concerns.

Zuckerberg appeared in front of the Senate commerce and judiciary committees on April 10, 2018. It did not go well. Zuckerberg showed up at the hearing looking like a high school kid in the middle of his sophomore slump. He appeared apathetic, uninterested, and uncaring. In the midst of questions from senators about serious allegations of ethics violations against Facebook, Zuckerberg seemed to shrug it off, as if he was thinking, "Eh, whatever." As the face of the brand, that's how Facebook looked to millions of people.

Zuckerberg is presiding over a sick culture. Facebook is an organization that has shown again and again that they won't take responsibility and, worse, that they don't care. There seems to be a level of arrogance that permeates from the top down. "We're Facebook, so whatever."

A few months later in July 2018, Facebook announced that it would miss revenue projections and that daily active user volume failed to meet expectations. In one day, Facebook shares fell by nearly 20 percent. That one-day plunge wiped out about $120 billion in market value. According to CNBC.com, "At least three analysts downgraded the stock after the report, and many on Wall Street raised concerns about the company's policies and forecast."

A sick corporate culture can be devastating to a company's long-term health.

NIKE'S TREATMENT OF WOMEN

Sick corporate cultures often involve gender discrimination and sexual harassment. According to an April 2018 article in the *New York Times*, Nike was among the worst corporate offenders in this regard. The newspaper reported that its journalists interviewed more than fifty current and former Nike employees and uncovered stunning accusations.

Women complained of being harassed by male coworkers and executives, marginalized and disrespected, hindered in their jobs, and blocked from career advancement. Specific complaints included forced visits to strip clubs with male coworkers and unwanted kissing. The *Times* wrote, "Many of those interviewed said when they took their grievances to human resources, they did not seem to be taken seriously." This is the very definition of a crisis of culture.

Then a group of women working at Nike decided to take action to force the company to acknowledge the way women are treated. They conducted an informal survey of female Nike employees to ask about their experiences with gender discrimination and sexual harassment. They presented the results of this survey to Nike CEO, Mark Parker, on March 5, 2018.

Less than two weeks later, a number of high-profile executives announced they were leaving Nike. In all, around a dozen male executives left in the wake of the scandal. According to the *New York Times*, "In his address to employees, Mr. Parker said that Nike was taking steps to become a more collaborative workplace where all voices were heard, and would be more open about efforts to improve the diversity of its work force and its progress toward meeting equal pay goals."

But the same questions that I asked about Wells Fargo still remain. How did this abuse happen right under the nose of senior management? Why did it go on so long? What kind of company treats its women employees so badly? Did this abusive attitude come from the CEO?

While all this was going on, Nike's marketing team was trying to align the brand more closely with the female market. They were launching women-only brands and products, and trying to grow their influence and leadership in women's sports by appealing to strong, athletic women. Talk about hypocrisy! This is a sign of a sick culture.

The difference between Nike and other companies who suffer brand crises is that Nike overall is a very strong brand. Nike is among the very best companies at branding, and they do a fantastic job of fostering an emotional connection between their loyal customer base and the

Nike brand. So I predict Nike will fully recover from this scandal.

But they must continue to prove to their customers and to the world that they take full responsibility, that they are accountable for what happened, that they are taking concrete steps to rectify the inequities of the past, and they are working to repair their corporate culture so something like this never happens again. Cleaning house of nearly a dozen top executives is certainly a good start, and it shows the world they're serious about fixing things.

Nike's leadership must continue to foster a culture where it's not enough to just say what the brand promise is. Every employee must live it in every single interaction at every touchpoint in the customer experience. Everyone in the company owns the brand. The brand is not just the job of the marketing department, the brand manager, or the CEO. The CEO is the leader and the driver. The CEO has the responsibility to equip everyone with the toolkit they need to be able to deliver on the promise of the brand.

This discussion of Nike leads us to ask why some brands can weather a crisis and others cannot. Just as when something bad happens in a marriage or a personal relationship, why can some relationships endure while others cannot? That is the topic of the next chapter.

One more thing...(see, I told you I can never stop talking about branding). In the wake of the Dr. David Dao debacle, United Airlines made some major changes. A friend who works for United told me that the airline will now authorize vouchers up to $10,000 in order to incentivize passengers to give up their seats and take a later flight. Ten thousand dollars! You didn't hear that from me. And it's just a rumor. Ten thousand dollars seems like a lot, but compared to a one-billion-dollar plunge in United stock, it's a small price to pay.

Chapter Six

YOU'RE GOING TO
STEP IN IT ANYWAY

Protests erupted after a seventeen-year-old African American man, Trayvon Martin, was fatally shot in Florida in February 2012. When the person who shot him, George Zimmerman, was acquitted of all charges, the hashtag #BlackLivesMatter spread across Twitter and other social media. The Black Lives Matter movement began to grow. It became well known for holding public demonstrations following the 2014 deaths of two more black men—Michael Brown in Ferguson, Missouri, and Eric Garner in New York City. Since then, BLM has expanded into an international organization that calls attention to and fights against violence and racism toward African Americans. BLM activists have taken on the serious life-and-death issues of racial inequality, criminal justice reform, racial profiling, and racially motivated police brutality against black men.

Apparently no one told Pepsi.

COULD YOU BE MORE TONE DEAF?

In 2017, at the height of the Black Lives Matter movement, some genius in Pepsi's marketing department thought it would be a good idea to market soft drinks off of the backs of the BLM protesters. Never mind the string of dead black kids at the hands of allegedly racist cops around the country. Never mind the real pain and human suffering that drives BLM protesters to show up and march in the streets. Never mind the often violent clashes between protesters and law enforcement. Screw it, let's sell some carbonated water and high fructose corn syrup!

Pepsi decided to shoot a commercial that recreated a street protest where activists confronted riot police— which critics viewed as a deliberate replica of a BLM march. Pepsi cast Kendall Jenner as the heroine who brings peace to the powder keg situation by handing one of the cops a can of Pepsi. Brilliant!

You can still watch the full commercial on YouTube. It's more than two-and-a-half minutes long, a mini-movie. The scenes are highly choreographed, beautifully lit, and the cinematography is majestic. It even tells a cute story. Jenner is in the middle of a photo shoot when she sees the angry protesters marching down the street toward a police barricade. In an effort to prevent a clash between the two groups, she hands a can of Pepsi to one of the cops. Smiles and happiness ensue on both sides. Awww, what's not to like?

Social media erupted in rage.

Memes and tweets eviscerated Pepsi for being so tone deaf as to try to sell product off the misery of dead black kids, and the activists who mourn them. Did Pepsi not realize that Black Lives Matter is a serious, committed movement that is trying to save the lives of African Americans? Was Pepsi not aware that they were indirectly promoting Kendall Jenner—who could be the poster girl for white privilege—as the face of BLM?

To make matters worse, the entire commercial was whitewashed and dripping in corporatized faux happiness. The protesters were smiling and high-fiving. They looked like they were straight from central casting, with perfectly white smiles. The happy-talk protest lacked any sense of the grittiness and gravity present in a real BLM march.

Pepsi had taken something real, visceral, and controversial, and whitewashed and sanitized it to look like a Coachella concert with John Mayer headlining. The whole thing stunk to high heaven of a corporation insensitively appropriating something that was going on in the news and trivializing the true human suffering at the root of the protests.

In the face of immediate and intense backlash, Pepsi at first defended the commercial. (The branding expert voice inside my head screamed, "No, Pepsi, no!") The company issued a statement saying, "This is a global ad that reflects people from different walks of life coming together in a spirit of harmony, and we think that's an important message to convey."

Face-palm.

Of course, that threw gasoline onto the fire. Within hours, Pepsi realized their error. They quickly got over their tone deafness and issued a proper statement, an apology. "Pepsi was trying to project a global message of unity, peace, and understanding. Clearly, we missed the mark, and we apologize. We did not intend to make light of any serious issue. We are removing the content and halting any further rollout. We also apologize for putting Kendall Jenner in this position."

Wow. Just wow. If PepsiCo, Inc., a multinational conglomerate with $63 billion in annual revenue across the globe and the best and brightest MBAs and marketing minds, can screw up this royally as a brand, *anyone* can. *You* can. And if you're in business long enough, you will. No matter how hard you try not to.

YOU WILL STEP IN IT

Practically every business will eventually step in it at some point. If you're in business long enough, there's no avoiding a branding mistake. It is so easy to make a mistake and have that mistake shared across the country and the world. That's why you have to honestly and authentically be in touch with your audience. You must think through how your actions will be perceived by the general public. That's the key to making sure your brand shows up the right way.

The Oscar for tone deaf startup of the year goes to Bodega. Two very smart ex-Google employees came up with an idea and raised a bunch of money through angel investors and a seed round. The concept was an automated version of the corner store, often called a bodega. Instead of going to the corner store, customers could use the mobile app to find the closest Bodega box, search through the inventory on their phone, then go to the box and take whatever they needed—soft drinks, snacks, toothpaste, cough medicine, toilet paper, and so on. Scanners on the Bodega box would automatically record the purchase and bill the customer's credit card.

"THAT IS NOT WHAT I ENVISIONED!"

One phenomenon that I've seen many times in marketing, especially in large companies, is the unfortunate transformation of a good idea into something awful after more and more people got involved in the creative. Here's a typical example. The creative department comes up with a clever idea for a campaign or an ad. Then the idea goes to a committee or is sent up to the executive suite for approval. Everyone weighs in with their opinion. Soon, the once-great idea devolves into something totally different. The magic of the original idea is lost. It's like that old saying, a camel is a horse designed by a committee.

I raise this concept in defense of Pepsi's marketing department. Their creative team is second to none. I don't know for sure, but it's very possible the original idea for the Kendall Jenner Pepsi spot was actually quite good. But after dozens of meetings and committees and executives weighed in, the concept may have completely changed into the cringeworthy disaster that everyone saw.

I can visualize the scene in my head. A bunch of VPs sitting around a huge conference table saying, "I don't want the protest to be too dark. Let's make it G-rated. Let's make sure everyone in the protest is smiling and smartly dressed so they look like they just stepped out of a Tide commercial."

"Good idea, Bob. Let's aim for protest-rally-meets-Hollywood-red-carpet, with lots of young, good-looking models with perfect teeth."

What may have begun as a good idea degenerated into a completely tone deaf finished product. In my mind, I can hear the creative who pitched the original idea screaming, "That is not what I envisioned!"

Not a bad idea, at least from a convenience perspective. But from a marketing perspective, it was a disaster. The magazine *Fast Company* interviewed the founders and timed their article to coincide with the Bodega's official launch. Here's the key line from the article, "The major downside to this concept—should it take off—is that it would put a lot of mom-and-pop stores out of business." In fact, the founders often bragged that their whole business model was to replace the corner store in neighborhoods across the country. They were proud of that goal.

Oops!

Talk about tone deaf. These two Google alums may be great coders or brilliant engineers, but they're god-awful marketers. Why? Because they built their entire business model on destroying thousands of family-owned small businesses that are very popular with their customers. People love their neighborhood corner stores. They are on a first-name basis with the owners—who are often immigrants who came to America with nothing and started a business. No one who frequents their family-owned corner store wants to see it put out of business, especially by two ex-Google entrepreneurs just so they can have a fifty-million-dollar exit.

Never has a startup launched with more negative buzz

than Bodega did. I can guarantee these two founders were not media trained before *Fast Company* interviewed them. They were probably so excited that *Fast Company* wanted to cover their launch that they failed to consider all the possible angles to this story. They never meant to step in it, but they sure did. And for a few weeks, it was the story that wouldn't go away.

Needless to say, the launch was shot. The company couldn't proceed in its current form. At last check, the founders were still pursuing the same basic business model, but they changed the name. According to an article on Eater.com, "Although Bodega seemed doomed from the start, somehow the Oakland, California-based business has persevered. And now, almost one year after their disastrous introduction to the world, the founders have finally decided to change the name to something less offensive (though rather forgettable): Stockwell."

In other words, same insufferable company, with a less tone deaf name. Meh. Can you tell I'm very protective of my local bodega?

VICTORIA'S SECRET KNOWS SEXY

Victoria's Secret is a global lingerie and fashion brand that is famous for the Victoria's Secret models—a bunch of tall, gorgeous, leggy young women who seem to do nothing but strut around fashion shows in their underwear and jet off to exotic locations to lie on the beach half-naked. Not bad work, if you can get it.

From a branding standpoint, it works because the brand is aspirational. Ninety-nine percent of women know they don't look like those models, but hey, if they put on a frilly ensemble from VS, they look damn good enough—if they do say so themselves.

From the start, Victoria's Secret has always been about making sexy accessible to the masses. Victoria's Secret stores are in practically every shopping mall in America. The brand is based in Columbus, Ohio, so appealing to women in Middle America has always been a focus. VS is *not* the brand for women who jet off to Paris twice a year to shop at La Perla.

In 2017, with all the best intentions, Victoria's Secret launched a campaign built around the phrase, "What is Sexy?" As a lingerie fashion house, they fancy themselves as an authority on what makes someone sexy. Unfortunately, the campaign was an epic branding disaster.

They launched the campaign around a piece of content that included a list of what Victoria's Secret endorses as sexy. In other words, a list of "What is sexy, *according to us*." When the list went public, critics in the media savaged Victoria's Secret. Mashable.com wrote, "Victoria's Secret, the world's most misguided authority on sexiness, released its annual 'What is Sexy' list, and (spoiler alert!) it's exactly what you think it is. Young, white, and thin."

It's one thing to create an aspirational brand that taps into the inner desire of the average-looking woman to feel sexy in whatever she wears. That's great. It's quite another thing to outwardly declare, "This is what sexy is. And oh, by the way, anyone who doesn't look this way (young, thin, and white) is not sexy." That campaign immediately insulted the vast majority of Victoria's Secret's audience, who are size eight and up. Whoops.

Customers want to see themselves in your brand, especially so with clothing and fashion brands. They want to see an acknowledgment of themselves in your products. Victoria's Secret built an entire campaign that basically said to the majority of their customers, "You're not sexy." That's a huge problem. That's a brand crisis.

There is no crisis of culture at VS; it's not a sick culture. There's no crisis of leadership; their CEO is just fine. Victoria's Secret never set out to offend anyone, but that was the end result. It was just a mistake. A lot of really smart people work for Victoria's Secret. Somehow, no one raised an alarm.

Believe it or not, Victoria's Secret never took the list down. You can still see it online. So not only did the brand step in it, but they never even scraped it off the bottom of their shoes.

JACK IN THE BOX FLOUTS THE ME TOO MOVEMENT

I've already talked about the Me Too movement earlier in this book. It's a huge phenomenon that seems to have engulfed the entire country. You'd have to be living in a dungeon not to be aware of how Me Too has shone a light on sexual harassment issues. Well, I guess no one told the marketing department at Jack in the Box restaurants.

Jack in the Box is known for edgy ad campaigns that push the envelope. But their teriyaki bowls campaign went too far, especially in the Me Too era.

The commercial begins with Jack, the character with the cartoon head, walking through the Jack in the Box offices. He says, "While other burger places serve the same old stuff, I'm the only one who has the *bowls* to serve something different." Obviously, the word "bowls" is being substituted for the word "balls." Later in the spot, Jack's male coworker says, "What about these bowls, Jack? Hey, you got some pretty nice bowls there. But so does Dan." Two female Jack in the Box employees are listening to this banter and they chime in, "Those are some nice bowls. Everyone's gonna want to get their hands on Jack's bowls."

You can't watch it without cringing. It's obvious to anyone that making overt puns about male genitalia *in the workplace, in front of female employees,* is not only offensive, it's also illegal. As a woman, this ad said to me that Jack in the Box is an organization that demeans women, is abusive to female employees, and thinks a hostile work environment is funny. It really offended me, and I'm not easily offended.

Think about the timing of this campaign. Jack in the Box went forward with it despite the massive public outcry against sexual harassment and sexual misconduct during the height of the Me Too movement. This has to be one of the most tone deaf campaigns ever. Even in another era, without the Me Too movement, it's still offensive.

Jack in the Box eventually issued a statement. They didn't apologize for offending anyone. They defended the spot. "As a brand known by its fans for its tongue-in-cheek, playful sense of humor, this ad is simply a creative and humorous expression around the teriyaki bowl product." Oooooo-kaaay. Thanks for pointing that out, I wasn't aware you were trying to be funny. The statement went on to say, "This ad is not diminishing any movement, and we stand firmly against any form of harassment and value those who have the guts to combat it." Yeah, not buying that.

This is an era where women are just starting to get brave about sharing these awful experiences. Jack in the Box mocked that concept by seemingly suggesting that it's okay in their workplace, even if it's a fictional workplace, to use obvious sexual innuendo to talk about bowls or balls all day long. To me, that means one thing: Jack in the Box is a brand I don't want to patronize, and it's certainly not a place where I would let my daughter work.

Having said that, I don't think the teriyaki bowls campaign will hurt Jack in the Box sales. Their core customer is probably males aged sixteen to twenty-five. This demographic is less likely to be offended by the sexual innuendo in the ads. They might actually think it's funny.

But is it worth it for Jack in the Box? What does an ad like this do for the long-term reputation of the brand? Is it worth getting some guilty laughs from young men but knowing your ads will offend millions of women, mothers, daughters, sisters, and wives? Only Jack in the Box can answer that.

IHOP GOES IHOB

The restaurant chain International House of Pancakes

has long promoted itself using the acronym IHOP. Customers know exactly what IHOP stands for and what type of food they serve. It's an established brand with more 1,600 restaurant locations worldwide. The IHOP logo is synonymous with light, fluffy pancakes cooked to perfection and other breakfast foods like eggs and sausage. The company is very profitable, and the logo is known around the world. Their website is IHOP.com.

So it was a surprise when IHOP announced in 2018 that the company was changing its name and logo to IHOb. The company began using the new IHOb logo on its website, in promotional materials, and on social media. The "b" in IHOb stands for "burgers." The goal was to draw attention to a new line of Angus beef specialty hamburgers.

Fans of the brand reacted with rage. People ranted on Twitter and Facebook that the company was turning its back on the product that made it famous—pancakes.

But it turns out the name change was a short-term publicity stunt designed to promote the new line of burgers. The company never had any intention of permanently changing the name. IHOP's CEO, Darren Rebelez, told Fortune.com, "We knew if we were going to really get into the burger business in a meaningful way that we were going to have to do something bold and creative.

We came up with the idea of flipping the 'P' to a 'b' to really grab everyone's attention."

While customers hated the temporary name change stunt, they sure talked about it a lot. For a few weeks, according to Rebelez, there were thousands of articles written about it, and millions of social media impressions. Rebelez said, "Literally everyone on the planet now knows we're in the burger business."

My take: it was a stupid stunt. It did generate word of mouth for a short time. But that word of mouth did not translate into increased purchase consideration. Just because people are talking about your brand when you pull a stunt doesn't mean they're going to be customers.

Just as with the Jack in the Box ad, companies need to think about whether a short-term boost in publicity for the brand is likely to pay off long term.

Brands try really, really hard not to screw up, but it happens anyway. It's a fact of life and part of human behavior. So when you are building and managing your brand, keep that in mind and try to prepare for the screw-ups that are inevitably going to come. They are uncontrollable, and plenty of branding disasters are no one's fault. The way to prepare is to build up enough positive equity in your brand's emotional bank account that it can survive any screw-up.

As in personal relationships, people sometimes make mistakes. When that happens, strong relationships survive. Relationships where two people have values and beliefs that are aligned can outlast any storm. When you know a person has a good heart, you can forgive occasional slip-ups.

Chapter Seven

SURVIVING BRAND DISASTERS

On April 12, 2018, two black men—Donte Robinson and Rashon Nelson—sat at a table in the Starbucks at Eighteenth and Spruce Streets in Philadelphia. They were waiting for a friend to have a business meeting. They had not purchased anything from the store. An employee asked them to leave the store. The men refused. A manager came over and asked them to leave. Again, the men refused.

The Starbucks store manager called the police. Several Philadelphia police officers arrived, and they also asked the men to leave. They refused. So the police officers arrested the men and marched them out of the store in handcuffs.

Several people in the store saw what was happening and began recording the incident. At least one person posted video of the arrest on Twitter. The video went viral and created nationwide outrage. Many posts on Twitter criticized Starbucks and the police for arresting the men for the crime of "sitting while being black."

Within a few days, the video racked up more than ten million views. Critics lobbed accusations of racial profiling at the police officers and of unconscious bias at the Starbucks manager. Social media blew up with the hashtag #BoycottStarbucks.

Starbucks's unfair and humiliating treatment of two black men suddenly blanketed every news outlet and TV station from coast to coast. This was not looking good for Starbucks.

MASTERFUL CRISIS COMMUNICATION

Starbucks's CEO, Kevin Johnson, instantly recognized the branding crisis that was spreading across the country. He knew he had to act fast. Unlike United Airlines, Starbucks immediately issued a written statement to apologize for the incident, apologize to the two men, take full accountability, and announce that Starbucks would be taking action to make sure this never happened again.

The statement that Johnson wrote is one of the best

pieces of crisis communication and brand management I've ever seen. Starbucks posted the letter—and a personal update video—on their website and social media accounts. In his video, which you can still watch on the website News.starbucks.com, Johnson takes full personal responsibility. He says, "There have been some calls for us to take action against the store manager. I believe that blame is misplaced. In fact, I think the focus of fixing this is I own it. This is a management issue, and I am accountable." Wow.

Johnson's initial written statement is so good, I am reprinting it here.

STARBUCKS CEO: REPREHENSIBLE OUTCOME IN PHILADELPHIA INCIDENT

Dear Starbucks Partners and Customers:

By now, you may be aware of a disheartening situation in one of our Philadelphia-area stores this past Thursday, that led to a reprehensible outcome.

I'm writing this evening to convey three things:

First, to once again express our deepest apologies to the two men who were arrested, with a goal of doing whatever we can to make things right. Second, to let you know of our plans to investigate the pertinent facts and make any necessary changes to our practices that would help prevent such an occurrence from ever happening again. And third, to reassure you that Starbucks stands firmly against discrimination or racial profiling.

In the coming days, I will be joining our regional vice president, Camille Hymes—who is on the ground in Philadelphia—to speak with partners, customers and community leaders as well as law enforcement. Most importantly, I hope to meet personally with the two men who were arrested to offer a face-to-face apology.

We have immediately begun a thorough investigation of our practices. In addition to our own review, we will work with outside experts and community leaders to understand and adopt best practices. The video shot by customers is very hard to watch and the actions in it are not representative of our Starbucks Mission and Values. Creating an environment that is both safe and welcoming for everyone is paramount for every store. Regretfully, our practices and training led to a bad outcome—the basis for the call to the Philadelphia police department was wrong. Our store manager never intended for these men to be arrested and this should never have escalated as it did.

We also will further train our partners to better know when police assistance is warranted. Additionally, we will host a company-wide meeting next week to share our learnings, discuss some immediate next steps and underscore our long-standing commitment to treating one another with respect and dignity. I know our store managers and partners work hard to exceed our customers' expectations every day—which makes this very poor reflection on our company all the more painful.

Finally, to our partners who proudly wear the green apron and to customers who come to us for a sense of community every day: You can and should expect more from us. We will learn from this and be better.

Respectfully,

Kevin Johnson

CEO

Shortly after issuing the statement, Johnson got on a plane and went to Philadelphia. He conducted interviews with local media in Philadelphia, and with national media including *Good Morning America*. He apologized and again called what happened to those two men reprehensible. He reiterated that he intended to apologize to the two men in person. He also met with local community leaders and government officials in Philadelphia.

Then a stunning announcement. Johnson declared that 8,000 Starbucks locations would close for a day so that 29,000 employees could attend unconscious bias and inclusion training. A simple back-of-the-envelope calculation multiplying 8,000 locations by the total daily revenue of the average Starbucks store quickly revealed this was an eight-figure decision for Starbucks. They were dead serious about making this right.

In a May 6, 2018, article, Forbes.com wrote, "Johnson did a very good job. His fellow CEOs, United's Oscar Munoz and Facebook's Mark Zuckerberg, recently faced a similar challenge and both failed to meet the bar that Johnson has now set. The inevitability and frequency of these events, immediately amplified by social media, seem to make apology skills part of a CEO's qualifications or at least preparation for the job."

Johnson did everything right. He acted swiftly and with

immediacy. He took full personal responsibility. He said he was accountable for what happened. He apologized to everyone. He never tried to blame the victims or even imply that they shared any blame. He said Starbucks would investigate what happened and get to the bottom of it. Then he announced a plan to ensure that nothing like this ever happens again. And finally, he reiterated Starbucks's brand promise and values.

Starbucks will not only survive this brand crisis, they will thrive, for two reasons. First, because their CEO handled the crisis appropriately and with great skill. Second, because Starbucks is already a strong brand to start with. Over the lifetime of the brand, they have invested significantly in building a solid foundation where everyone in the company understands and lives the organization's core values. Starbucks's leaders hire, manage, and reward their employees based on those values. The Starbucks brand will be able to withstand any brand crisis. Starbucks is a brand that's going to endure because it's a brand that has a set of core values and beliefs and lives them every day.

DISASTER STRIKES SOUTHWEST

The worst type of disaster that any organization can face is when someone is seriously injured or dies. Strong brands with solid brand values will respond accordingly.

In Chapter 1, we talked about how Southwest Airlines held a flight so they could get a passenger home to a dying loved one. That demonstrated strong brand values. But those values would soon be tested in the face of a fatal aviation disaster on a Southwest jet.

On April 17, 2018, Southwest flight 1380 took off from LaGuardia Airport on its way to Dallas. Shortly after take-off, one of the jet engines failed. Debris from the engine struck the fuselage of the Boeing 737, damaging a cabin window and causing rapid depressurization of the cabin. The loss of cabin pressure sucked a passenger partially out the window, and she later died. Eight other passengers suffered injuries. This was the first deadly accident on a Southwest jet.

Southwest is a brand built on the values of love, respect, and regard for humanity and caring for its customers. Their stock symbol is LUV, for goodness' sake. Even under stressful conditions, Southwest employees maintain their cool and do their best to accommodate passengers in an upbeat, loving, and respectful way. Leadership has done an outstanding job of making sure every Southwest employee lives, eats, and sleeps those values.

As a result, this is a brand that can withstand the worst kind of disaster and still come through with an incredibly strong brand reputation. They can even reinforce their brand's relationship with customers by how they show up in a crisis.

And Southwest showed up big time. As soon as the damaged plane landed, the pilot walked up and down the aisles talking to passengers, apologizing, listening, and reassuring them. Meanwhile, the airline's emergency response plan was already in motion. Step one was to ensure the safety of all Southwest passengers and flights. Crews fanned out across the country to inspect every engine and fan blade to make sure they were not at risk of failure.

According to an article on DallasNews.com, "The company's top priority, [Southwest CEO Gary] Kelly said, has been taking care of those who were on the flight, a challenge the carrier has seemingly risen to meet, based on praise from many of those onboard. In the days since, Southwest employees have been in regular contact by phone and email with the passengers. On Wednesday, the company provided $5,000 to each to help cover immediate expenses in an email signed by Kelly that began, 'On behalf of the entire Southwest Airlines family, please accept our sincerest apologies.'"

STRONG BRANDS LIVE THEIR VALUES

The strongest brands are clear on their values and live

those values. They hire, train, and incentivize their employees based on those values. They maintain customer relationships according to those values. They make sure there is alignment with those values at every level of the organization. Their marketing promotes and is consistent with those values. Brands that do this can withstand any crisis.

In relationship terms, when you have a foundation of shared values and shared beliefs and something that you stand for as a couple or as a family, you can develop those conditions of unconditional love and loyalty. Your beliefs and values are aligned. That's what the Starbucks and Southwest stories show us.

Having a foundation of strong brand values does not, however, negate the need for a proper apology when a brand screws up. Both are required. From what I have observed in my career in branding, it is the *combination* of strong brand values *plus* an artful apology that prevails after a brand disaster.

The same holds true for personal relationships. When my partner and I have an argument, or one of us does something that hurts the other, we always get past it. First, we offer a sincere, heartfelt apology—ideally combined with a promise not to do it again. Second, underpinning that apology is our strong emotional bond and shared values—the foundation of our relationship. The combination of those two elements (apology + values alignment) will help any personal relationship endure a crisis.

Not sure how to master the art of the apology? Check out the sidebar. When your brand steps in it, pull out this sidebar and follow the steps.

THE ART OF THE BRAND APOLOGY

There is nothing more insulting than a half-hearted, "Sorry, not sorry" fake apology, except perhaps a fake apology that blames someone else, or God forbid, blames the victim. Yet brands do it all the time. As a result, they piss off their customers even worse than if they had said nothing at all.

If you apologize sincerely, if you do it quickly and you do it right, then you can mitigate disaster. But there are important elements to any brand apology. Follow the steps below, and your apology will be well received.

First, take action right away to acknowledge that damage was done to another person or group. Do not delay. Do not take a wait-and-see attitude. Do not let fear paralyze you. Do not get defensive. Get out in front of any potential social media or public backlash.

Second, the top leader of the organization must accept full, unconditional, personal responsibility for what happened. Don't delegate the apology to a VP. The buck stops with the CEO.

Third, own the offense, admit fault, and be sincere. Even if it makes you squirm. Apology is a place where you have to strip yourself psychologically naked and be raw and vulnerable. Mean it when you say it. When you apologize, feel sorry in your heart. Don't say, "I'm sorry your feelings got hurt." That's hedging. Speak or write in the first person and avoid passive voice. Say, "I'm sorry I hurt your feelings." Don't try to offer excuses. Never blame the victim. Own it.

Fourth, acknowledge the impact your actions had on the other person or persons. Never try to minimize what the people affected by your actions may or may not have felt, because you don't know.

Fifth, don't offer too much explanation. Keep explanations short and relevant, and above all, don't use them as justification for your actions.

Sixth, explain what you're going to do about it. How is leadership going to implement new policies or change things in the organization to ensure that this never happens again? If you promise to make changes in the organization, follow through on those promises.

And finally, clearly restate the bedrock values and beliefs of the brand. Acknowledge that you missed the mark this time, then recommit to living up to those values in the future. A branding disaster can sometimes be an opportunity to reinforce what your brand stands for.

Chapter Eight

BRANDS THAT DID EXACTLY THE RIGHT THINGS FOR THEIR CUSTOMERS

Dalmatians riding on horse-drawn carriages full of Budweiser. The latest hot new flavor of Doritos. Morgan Freeman drinking an ice-cold Mountain Dew while rapping Missy Elliott lyrics. A star-studded Amazon ad featuring celebrities like Anthony Hopkins and Gordon Ramsay filling in for the voice of Alexa. I'm one of those people who cares more about the commercials during every Super Bowl broadcast than I do about watching the actual football game. And Super Bowl LII in 2018 did not disappoint.

But while most Super Bowl party guests watch the ads in search of a good laugh or a touching *awww* moment, I'm paying attention to the branding and key messaging. I'm trying to determine the ideal customer these brands are appealing to with their multi-million-dollar commercials. One Super Bowl commercial in particular caught my eye. In fact, it caught the eye of many people, and riled up some fervent criticism.

WeatherTech is an Illinois-based manufacturing company that makes after-market accessories primarily for trucks and SUVs. Mud flaps, all-weather floor mats, pickup truck bedliners, cargo nets, dog cages, and so on. It's not difficult to figure out who their ideal customer is—hard-working men in Middle America who work in construction, farming, ranching, manufacturing, or who just like pickup trucks and muddy dirt roads. In other words, the archetypal Donald Trump supporter.

In a sea of celebrity-centric Super Bowl commercials driven by A-list actors and Hollywood directors, the WeatherTech ad stood out like a muddy F-150 on the showroom floor of a Beverly Hills Ferrari dealership. The ad featured a series of documentary-style video clips of construction workers building the new WeatherTech factory in Bolingbrook, Illinois. There were shots of cement trucks, welders, cranes, concrete slabs, bulldozers, and lots of bearded men wearing hard hats and tool belts. And

prominently featured with the sun shining through it...
the American flag.

No voiceover. Hardly any music. Just the sights and
sounds of hardworking Americans building a giant factory in Illinois. At the end of the spot, two short sentences
appeared in print. "At WeatherTech, we built our new factory right here in America. Isn't that the way it's supposed
to be?" The ad proudly displayed very obvious support for
Donald Trump's policies. It was an overtly political spot
but done in a thoughtful and authentic way.

The ad set off a firestorm on Twitter. Some people absolutely hated it. They saw it as an obvious endorsement
of Donald Trump's Make America Great Again ethos.
Progressives rejected the ads as ethnocentric and geo-
centric, and the opposite of being inclusive, globalist, or
diverse. The ad was the antithesis of many of the other
Super Bowl ads in 2018, in which brands touted diversity,
inclusion, equality, political activism, and other social
justice causes—in other words, opposition to the policies
of Donald Trump.

As a viewer watching one Super Bowl ad after another
showcasing political correctness swaddled in Hollywood
glitz, I found the WeatherTech ad almost a shock to the
system. Its message was contrary to almost every other ad.
So it's no wonder so many on Twitter reacted with scorn.

At the Super Bowl party I attended, I heard several people moan in disgust after seeing the ad. One person said something like, "Well that company just shot itself in the foot." But did it? Was the contrarian WeatherTech ad a fail?

Absolutely not.

Even though I was already three Chardonnays in to the party (okay, four), I could still recognize the tactical brilliance of the WeatherTech ad. The WeatherTech marketing team didn't design it to appeal to coastal yuppies who live in New York, Washington, San Francisco, or Los Angeles. They designed it to directly target WeatherTech customers in the heartland.

The message of keeping jobs in America, reinvesting in American manufacturing, building factories, working hard, driving trucks, and making America great resonated perfectly with the intended audience. WeatherTech directly aligned its brand with the policies of Donald Trump. Whether you like Donald Trump or not, the ad was strategic, it hit the mark for that brand's ideal customers, and it was a home run for the WeatherTech brand.

ONE SIZE DOES NOT FIT ALL

The WeatherTech story illustrates the idea that all brands

do not share the same set of values and beliefs. WeatherTech customers drive pickup trucks and live in the heartland. Companies that serve customers in big cities on the East and West Coast will demonstrate different values than WeatherTech. I always come back to the idea that brands are like magnets. They have a set of values and beliefs that attracts customers who share those values and beliefs.

That's why brands need to have a point of view. That point of view needs to be distinctive and deliberately focused on the type of people they're trying to attract to the brand. Hence, there is a different strategy for every brand.

If one size fit all in branding, every company would be saying the same thing. But they're not. Every brand is unique and must align with its customers in the best way to reach that specific target audience. When brands do that, the brand will strengthen its relationship with customers.

Branding strategy is about figuring out whom exactly your brand is for, and then creating a brand around that person. Who is your ideal customer? What is the ideal customer archetype or avatar? Which specific customer is going to be the most profitable and a delight to serve? Who is going to buy from you again and again?

MGM'S ILL-TIMED AD CAMPAIGN

Two weeks before the deadliest mass shooting in US history, MGM Resorts unveiled an epic new ad campaign. Their marketing team had been working on it for a year and a half. The campaign tagline was, "Welcome to the Show." Unfortunately, many of the TV spots also included the line, "Blow the minds of all mankind."

Two weeks later, on October 1, 2017, a gunman in a hotel room at the Mandalay Bay opened fire. He rained more than a thousand bullets down on innocent concert goers at the Route 91 Harvest Music Festival across the street. Fifty-eight people died. More than 800 suffered serious injuries.

Clearly, an ad campaign that includes the line, "Blow the minds of all mankind," instantly became not just insensitive, but offensive. Despite having spent a year and a half and millions of dollars on it, MGM immediately pulled the ads and scrapped the entire campaign. Smart move.

In place of the "Welcome to the Show" campaign, MGM rapidly pulled together a new idea. Just a few weeks later, they unveiled the new spot during *Saturday Night Live* on NBC. They called it, "Together We Shine."

The thirty-second commercial featured scenic shots of Las Vegas interspersed with the short captions, "Together we are one," "Together we rise," and, "Together we shine." MGM set the visuals to background music, the song, "This Little Light of Mine." At the end of the spot, a small title card fades in that says, "MGM Resorts," followed by "#VegasStrong." You can see the spot on YouTube.

The spot reinforced that MGM is part of the Las Vegas community. It communicated sadness about the tragedy, but also a desire to show support and a determination to bounce back. It was dignified. It helped promote the Vegas Strong movement. Even though the spot mentioned MGM briefly at the end, it very much represented the sentiment of the Las Vegas community. It absolutely did *not* come off as MGM co-opting a tragedy to selfishly promote its own brand profile.

Lili Tomovich, an MGM executive, told BusinessInsider. com, "We created this spot to reflect the strength and resilience of Las Vegas, of MGM Resorts, of Mandalay Bay, and of all of our employees. It reinforces our promise to the world that we'll remain strong and united in the face of adversity." This was a brand that did something right. MGM did something to help others through its branding.

Despite MGM's good intentions, people criticized MGM for coming out with an ad campaign so soon after the tragedy. But from a branding standpoint, I thought it was great. By addressing the shooting promptly and adapting its message to reflect the tragedy, the brand not only avoided potentially taking a tone-deaf stance but also demonstrated that its values align with those of its customers. The spot is quietly dignified, prioritizes the master brand and sentiment of the Vegas hospitality community above its own, and represents an idea that transcends merely selling hotel rooms.

MGM showed how quickly brands sometimes need to react to a sudden event or drastic change in the market. You never know what disaster or news story is going to shift public attitudes and opinions—sometimes in a matter of just a few hours. What's important is that strong brands react the right way. MGM's response was classy, appropriate, tasteful, and effective. Their response demonstrated their brand values, and their customers surely appreciated their sensitivity to such a tragic event.

I admired what MGM did here. It was meaningful. It was unifying. It was classy. And they executed it beautifully.

DICK'S SPORTING GOODS

Just a few months after the Las Vegas mass shooting, tragedy struck again, this time in Parkland, Florida. A teenage gunman began shooting inside Stoneman Douglas High School, killing seventeen students and staff. The shooter injured more than a dozen others. The incident is the deadliest high school shooting in US history.

Antigun activists were already calling for stricter gun control laws after the Las Vegas shooting, and the Parkland tragedy increased support for such measures. In addition, several students who survived the massacre became vocal proponents of more gun control. They also began calling for boycotts of companies that worked with the National Rifle Association.

Regardless of which side you fall on in the gun control debate, that consumer pressure began to take hold. Merchants and brands were seeing customers moving away from companies that do business with the NRA or that sell or finance guns.

One of the brands that responded was Dick's Sporting Goods. Back in 2012, after the Sandy Hook shooting, Dick's had already stopped selling semi-automatic AR-15-style rifles in their stores. After the Parkland shooting, they decided to pull these rifles from all thirty-five of their Field & Stream stores. Dick's also raised the minimum age to buy a gun in their stores to twenty-one, and they banned high-capacity magazines.

A written statement on the Dick's website explained, "We support and respect the Second Amendment, and we recognize and appreciate that the vast majority of gun owners in this country are responsible, law-abiding citizens. But we have to help solve the problem that's in front of us. Gun violence is an epidemic that's taking the lives of too many people, including the brightest hope for the future of America—our kids."

The outcry from Second Amendment advocates was immediate. They criticized Dick's for caving to public pressure. They predicted that Dick's would alienate so many customers that they'd go out of business. They said Dick's is going to fail.

I completely disagree. As a branding move, Dick's gun restrictions were savvy.

The gun control debate was national news every day after the Parkland shooting. Soccer moms across the country had night terrors thinking about an active shooter at their kids' schools. There's nothing that will get a suburban mama bear with school-age kids more wound up than talking about making guns available to people who could potentially harm their children. Who hates guns more than moms with kids? No one.

Now guess who the ideal customer is for Dick's. It's not elk and antelope hunters. It's not Navy SEALs or US Marines. It's soccer moms!

Dick's decision to take a stand and limit gun sales may have disgruntled a small percentage of their customers (gun buyers). But it likely thrilled their core customers, women with school-age children who buy shin guards, baseball gloves, track shoes, and soccer balls.

Serious firearms enthusiasts who buy guns and ammo in volume don't shop at Dick's anyway. So from a branding standpoint, Dick's made a smart decision. They know who their customers are and what their values are. By limiting gun sales in their stores, Dick's more closely aligned their values with their core customers' values.

This is another example, similar to Nike signing Colin Kaepernick, in which a brand took a stand that angered some of its customers. Once again, the brand made the right decision. Dick's put their values on display, took a stand, and decided to stand with their best customers.

PASS THE TIDE PODS

Dick's made the right call by responding to public pressure. But that isn't always the best strategy. Sometimes it just doesn't make sense for a brand to go along with unreasonable public demands. Especially for established brands with rock solid values and a strong brand promise that is beyond reproach.

Procter and Gamble's Tide detergent is a good example. P&G makes the infamous Tide Pods—cute, brightly-colored little packets that look like a cross between gummy bears and powdered Pixy Stix. In other words, they look like a delicious candy or a snack food. So it's not surprising that P&G warns parents to keep Tide Pods away from small children.

I can easily see how small children could mistake the pods for food and ingest one or two. But surely teenagers know better than to eat *laundry detergent*. Um...nope. They don't. One of the recent YouTube viral video sensations running rampant among teenagers is something called the Tide Pod Challenge. This is where young people desperate for fame or conformity eat Tide Pods on video and hope for maximum views and likes.

The problem is that Tide is a bunch of cleaning chemicals and you can get really sick or even die from eating it. As more and more dimwitted teens posted videos of themselves taking the Tide Pod Challenge, parents became indignant. They saw the challenge as a major public health risk and demanded that P&G take action. Some parents insisted that P&G remove the product from store shelves. Others begged P&G to reformulate the product so that it wouldn't make teens sick if they ingested it.

Well, P&G's response was not exactly what angry parents were hoping for. The company has one of the best reputations for health and safety in the country. P&G has a well-known and rock-solid brand promise of being a trustworthy, reliable, safe consumer products company that values family and children. Tide Pods already come with multiple written warnings, and P&G has produced public service campaigns about safe and responsible use of the product.

Nevertheless, many parents of teens who took the Tide Pod Challenge were shocked at P&G's response. In a written statement on their website, CEO David Taylor wrote the following:

> As my kids became teens, they naturally sought more freedom in their lives to do things like drive, go out with friends and stay out later. My job of ensuring their safety increasingly became more about teaching them what it means to behave responsibly so they could make good decisions on their own.
>
> As a father, seeing recent examples of young people intentionally take part in self-harming challenges like ingesting large amounts of cinnamon or the so-called "Tide Pods Challenge" is extremely concerning.
>
> The possible life altering consequences of this act, seeking internet fame, can derail young people's hopes and dreams and ultimately their health.

Ensuring the safety of the people who use our products is fundamental to everything we do at P&G. However, even the most stringent standards and protocols, labels and warnings can't prevent intentional abuse fueled by poor judgment and the desire for popularity.

In other words, "Parents, this is on you. You need to learn some parenting skills and police your own damn kids."

Many people felt offended by P&G's response. But they also knew the CEO was right. A company can only put so many warnings on product packaging. At some point, teenagers have to use common sense and be accountable for their own actions. After all, most homes have a whole bunch of caustic cleaning supplies under the sink, and teens aren't eating or drinking that stuff on YouTube.

P&G has a nearly two-hundred-year history of providing safe consumer products. No one is questioning their integrity or their values. So the CEO decided not to cave in to consumer pressure. P&G refused to pull the product off store shelves. Instead, their statement basically said, "We're P&G. Look at our reputation. We stand for safety, which has always been our priority. Tide Pods are a safe and effective product when used properly. Parents, control your own kids."

P&G's response was right on the money. They were well

within their rights to respond that way, and it was the right thing for the brand to do. A lesser known brand without such a strong brand promise and without a long track record of safe products might not be able to get away with a statement like that. But for P&G, it worked.

When you're managing your brand, stay true to your brand strategy. Stay true to your target audience, stay true to your brand legacy, and stay true to your brand foundation. Don't waver on your principles just because some people are making public demands. It is often when brands waiver that they behave in a way that is inconsistent with their values. That's when customers get confused. The way P&G responded by pushing back against public pressure actually made the brand look stronger, not weaker.

TIKI TORCH NAZIS

In Chapter 3, I mentioned the Charlottesville, Virginia, march by white supremacists and the protesters who opposed them. There's a fascinating branding story that arose out of that event. And it has to do with, of all things, Tiki Torches.

When that group of white supremacists marched through Charlottesville, I guess they didn't think they were quite creepy enough, so they tried to crank up the creepy factor by carrying torches. Yes, long sticks with flames on the top. Did they carve custom-made torches out of birch wood? Nope. That takes too much effort. They carried whatever kind of torches they could buy at the local Target store. Tiki brand torches, to be exact.

The news footage of a group of white supremacists marching through the streets carrying Tiki Torches was eerie and disturbing to millions of people watching around the country. But it was acutely disturbing to the small Wisconsin town of Menomonee Falls. That's where Lamplight Farms Incorporated is located—the owner of Tiki Brands and the manufacturer of Tiki Torches.

For Lamplight Farms, the only thing more horrifying than watching white supremacists endorsing the Tiki brand on television all over the country, was reading the headlines the next day. CNN.com published the headline, "White Nationalists Use Tiki Torches to Light Up Charlottesville March." Other news outlets wrote headlines like, "Tiki Torches, Terror, and Tears." *Forbes* wrote a piece titled, "A Short History of Torches and Intimidation."

If you work at Lamplight Farms, those headlines are enough to make you drink. And maybe call your lawyer. To make matters much, much worse, soon the hashtag #TikiTorchNazis began trending on social media.

Out of nowhere, without warning, and through absolutely no fault of their own, the Tiki brand stepped in it big time. The company found itself not only thrust into a national debate about racism, but also smothered in the stench of hate speech and white supremacy on the cover of every newspaper and news site in America.

Not good.

The company immediately began scrambling to set the record straight. They had to tell the world that they are not a racist company and they have absolutely no connection to white supremacists. On Twitter, Facebook, the company website, and everywhere possible, Lamplight Farms posted the following statement.

> TIKI Brand is not associated in any way with the events that took place in Charlottesville and we are deeply saddened and disappointed. We do not support their message or the use of our products in this way. Our products are designed to enhance backyard gatherings and to help family and friends connect with each other at home in their yard.

On Facebook, people shared the statement nearly 10,000 times, posted nearly 1,000 comments, and hit the like button 13,000 times. It's still at the top of the company's Facebook homepage.

As a result, the Tiki brand took a really, really bad brand crisis and turned it into an opportunity. They knew their name would continue to be written and talked about by the mass media for at least another week or two, so they used the free publicity to reinforce what they really do stand for as a brand. The last sentence of their statement says it all: "Our products are designed to enhance backyard gatherings and to help family and friends connect with each other at home in their yard." That is a clear statement of what their brand values are. In other words, our brand is about backyard fun, not hating people because of their skin color.

I like that they made a very strong stand as a brand. I think, ultimately, it gave their brand a big boost. I know I went out and bought some Tiki products for my home. I'll never buy any other brand.

IT'S ALWAYS ABOUT THE IDEAL CUSTOMER

The reason I like these branding stories is that they remind us to focus on one thing, the ideal customer. In branding, it always, always goes back to the ideal customer. One hundred percent of the time. Know who your ideal customer is. Then you build the brand for that archetypal customer.

When you aim your brand at that one ideal customer, you

can build momentum. Every time you communicate in a consistent way with your ideal customers, you create those conditions of irrational loyalty.

Chapter Nine

BUILD A BRAND THAT THRIVES

I was single up until a few years ago. In one year, I went out on seventy-two dates with different people. That's 1.4 dates a week. I went out with some pretty amazing men who looked great on paper. I went out with doctors, lawyers, politicians, athletes, authors, and CEOs. All had impressive résumés, and they looked great on the internet. OK, on Tinder.

I even went out with a commercial fisherman, who was fascinating. But no matter how attractive they looked on paper or in person, none of them connected with me on a deep emotional level because our values and beliefs didn't line up. So I didn't end up in a long-term relationship with any of them.

Similarly, from a branding perspective, many brands look good on paper. They're attractive. They look nice. I was intrigued enough to give it a try. But in the end, they never hooked me in that deeply connected, emotional way that bonds me to them so that I become irrationally loyal.

It's easy to build a brand that looks good on paper and shows up smartly dressed on a first date. It is much better to create a brand that connects on a deeper level. The goal is to build a brand that customers are going to fall in love with, stay in love with, and grow deeper in love with as time goes on. Brands that can do that will be able to survive any crisis.

Put another way, some organizations build a brand to sell; others build brands to *bond*. You should always strive to build brands that bond with customers. Recall the story of Blue Bell ice cream at the beginning of this book. They built a brand to bond, and they created irrational loyalty among their customers.

Irrational loyalty exists when customers are so dedicated to a certain brand that their lives would be diminished if that product disappeared. Irrational loyalty means customers wouldn't even consider using an alternative brand. The way brands build irrational loyalty among their customers is by bonding emotionally.

SEPHORA VS. MACY'S

When I walk past a Sephora store, I'm always struck that it's the only store in the mall that's as crowded as the Apple store. It looks like a cosmetics wonderland, a makeup amusement park. There are mirrors and free samples everywhere. The lights remind me of a movie star's dressing room. Professional makeup artists wearing holsters full of brushes roam the aisles, encouraging customers to experiment and try new looks. They practically force you to put on makeup.

The whole branding message of Sephora is, "Come in and play." And people do by the hundreds. Every Sephora store I've ever been in is packed with customers. It's a brand that fully engages and immerses its customers in the experience. Sephora has created a brand that people want to *use*.

Go visit the makeup section of a Macy's department store. Fluorescent lighting casts a white glow on the glass makeup cases. All the makeup is locked up, out of reach. No touching. You have to ask for someone to help you. You have to beg someone to let you try on makeup. The sales lady is your mom's age, and she's wearing what looks like a white lab coat. The store is oddly silent, even though elevator music plays. Who knew you could turn a Cold Play song into an acoustic-only version with just strings?

Macy's and Sephora sell the same products from the same brands. Yet the experience of each could not be more different. Macy's is a strong national brand. But it's a brand designed to sell Macy's. In contrast, Sephora is a brand built to make customers want to *use* it.

If you're building a brand, make sure you build a brand that people want to use. Build a brand that customers want to have a long-term relationship with. Build a brand whose values and beliefs align with that ideal customer. Be the Sephora brand. Don't be the Macy's brand.

When you have that really tight alignment with customers and you have a strong bond in the relationship, you don't just want to take a roll in the hay with somebody. You become loyal to that person. You want to go through all of life's trials and tribulations with that person. The same goes for brands.

HOW TO BUILD A BRAND PEOPLE WANT TO USE

My previous book *Branding Is Sex* laid out the process for building a brand that customers will want to use. It is a how-to book. Ultimately, that process is about making your customer the hero in their own story.

Whom do you have the best relationships with? You have the best relationships with the people who are part of your own hero story. Those people make you look good. They make you feel good about yourself. They elevate your self-concept. As a result, they are the people you form the strongest bonds with.

Making a brand look good in superficial marketing and flashy commercials doesn't cut it. You have to build a brand that becomes part of someone's self-concept. The products we buy, the clothes we wear, the stores we shop at, are all part of the story that we are creating for ourselves.

The first step on the way to irrational loyalty is to ask the three magical brand questions.

1. **What does it say about a person that they use this brand?** It's important to note how I worded this question. What does it say about a person that they *use* this brand, not that they *buy* this brand. Those can be two different things. Use is a much stronger predictor of indispensability. How many products have you purchased that you never use? How many outfits sit in your closet with the tags still on? You get the idea. Focus on building a brand that people are going to love to *use*.

2. **What is the singular thing that they get from us that they can't get anywhere else?** That thing is never just a clever marketing campaign. Those are

a dime a dozen. That thing is not a fancy Super Bowl ad. We see those by the dozens every year. Marketing and commercials are just tools to sell the brand. The singular thing comes from the experience of actually using the brand. If you focus on building a brand that is singular and indispensable, it will always be meaningful to that ideal customer.

3. **How do we make our customer the hero in their own story?** This is the most important of the three questions. As I explain in *Branding Is Sex*, this question boils down to how does your brand get your customers laid? It has nothing to do with a streamlined sales process or creative marketing. It goes back to the building blocks of a brand. Getting your customers laid is the key to building a brand that can engender that deep emotional connection that leads to irrational loyalty.

FOCUS ON WHAT CUSTOMERS SAY TO OTHERS

More important than what a brand says to its customers is what those customers say to others about the brand. If you build a brand that's designed to be used, then people will use it. They will experience the benefit of it. It will elevate their self-concept and turn them into brand advocates. Pretty soon, they will be recommending the brand to all their friends.

The common thread in all three questions is that customers must *use* the brand. Always build a brand to use, not to sell.

AIRBNB

Airbnb is a good example of a brand that's built to use versus a brand that's built to sell. Why did Airbnb grow so big so fast? Because they built something that solves a very particular problem for people, so customers want to use it. Airbnb changed the hospitality model and created a different experience for customers in a way that hotels could never match.

Staying in someone's home while you're on vacation feels very different than checking into the Marriott. It allows travelers to more fully experience what life is like for the locals. Airbnb customers can travel on their own terms, instead of having those terms dictated by the corporate hotel chain. Airbnb lets you be more of a traveler and less of a tourist. Airbnb built a brand that people want to use.

DOLLAR SHAVE CLUB

Consider the difference between Dollar Shave Club and buying a pack of razors at Walgreens. Dollar Shave Club took a neglected product category and turned the model on its ear. Instead of the hassle of going to the local drugstore and waiting in line to buy shaving supplies, Dollar Shave Club created a way to have an ongoing relationship with customers.

Just sign up on the website, answer a few questions, and then a box of shaving supplies shows up on your doorstep so you never run out. You never have to drive to Walgreens at eight in the morning because you ran out of shaving cream before your big presentation. DSC makes shaving fun again. DSC is fun to *use*.

Who knew that an entire business model could be built around this in a way that would revolutionize the ecommerce industry forever? It's because Dollar Shave Club built a brand that was targeted at an ideal customer, solved a very particular problem for them, and made it freaking cool to shave again.

Not to mention, it gave people bragging rights just for being a customer. There is a level of pride in being a Dollar Shave Club member. I don't know about you, but I've never heard anyone bragging about going to RiteAid and waiting in line to buy a ten-pack of Gillette razors.

VENMO

When credit cards became mainstream, they brought a whole new world of convenience to payment processing.

They revolutionized the finance industry. Now we're entering the next frontier of payments, and a popular app called Venmo is leading the way. With Venmo, you can pay anybody with a few taps on your smartphone. It's a cool, fun, and social way to split the bill at a restaurant with friends or to pay off your gambling debts with your bookie. Users can even share, like, and comment on payments. "Next time, I'm taking the Steelers plus the points!"

Venmo has grown its user base without spending money on advertising. They've done zero marketing. The company's growth has come entirely through building a brand to use. People try it once, and they want to use it again and again. It's fun.

When is the last time you had fun paying with a credit card? Venmo is so easy and simple, I wonder if credit cards are even going to be around in ten years. Venmo is a product people love to use.

Ultimately, if you're building a brand that has any kind of a viral strategy, you must build something that's designed to be used. When people use it, they will experience the benefit of it, it will elevate their self-concept, and that will turn them into brand advocates. That experience will turn them into legions of irrationally loyal fans who are proud of the fact that they use your brand and will want to share that with others.

The only way you can get that word-of-mouth support and use your customers as a legion of marketers for your brand is by creating something that your customers really want to use.

ACTIONS SPEAK LOUDER THAN MARKETING

It's easy to brag about your company values to your customers. It's an entirely different thing to actually walk the talk. At the core of any brand, what matters most is that you as an organization believe in your brand and that you're willing to do the hard things associated with delivering on your brand promise.

One of my favorite examples of a brilliantly executed brand promise is Ritz-Carlton Hotels. Ritz-Carlton's brand promise is, "We are ladies and gentlemen serving ladies and gentlemen." Every interaction customers have with that brand is absolutely impeccable and beyond compare to any other luxury hotel and resort brand. That's because this is a brand that has completely bought into the brand promise from the top down. Every single person in the company is not only indoctrinated into it but rewarded, incentivized, coached, managed, and hired through the lens of that brand promise.

The way to build a brand that people want to use is through consistent actions that align with the brand promise, then staying focused on delivering on your brand promises with every single interaction.

When we look at some of the strongest brands in the world—Coca-Cola, Pepsi, Google, Amazon, Apple, Oracle, SAP—they all have one thing in common. They built really strong brands by aiming at an ideal customer, that North Star customer. These are brands that elevate their users' self-concept through the use of those brands. They make each of their customers a hero in their own story, and they broadcast that to the world.

Above all, these are brands with strong beliefs and values, and they align all their behavior as a brand with those beliefs and values. They're clear, consistent, current, and relevant in delivering on their brand promise. And they do so on an ongoing basis.

Follow the principles in this book, and your brand can create irrational loyalty just like those marquee brands.

CONCLUSION

My goal with this book is to inspire people to build a brand that doesn't just attract customers in the short term but keeps them in a long-term, constructive, value-added relationship. Part of that goal is my personal mission to create a billion dollars of financial value through helping companies create rock-solid brands and build irrational customer loyalty.

At Sol Marketing, my staff and I have a deep love for branding. We thrive on creating wins for brands because when one of our client's brands wins, we all win. We transform things. It's as if we change them from a solid state to liquid to vapor. We're transforming matter through the process of branding.

It is not easy. We do hard things. The process of branding

is hard. There is no way around that. As the leader of a company, the president of an organization, the head of marketing, a solopreneur, or the founder of a nonprofit who is trying to make an impact on the world, you have to be willing to do the hard work of branding.

I tell clients at the outset, "You have to really have the stomach for this because we are going to transform your business through the process of branding. When I say transform, I mean we're going to change its very state of matter." Some company leaders get scared off by that.

Any process of transformation is going to require pain. There's going to be bloodshed. At the end of the process, when you emerge with a reignited strategic brand strongly aligned with the values and beliefs of your ideal customer, you're going to have employees or other leaders at the company who don't buy in.

They're going to have to leave.

They'll either self-select out, or you're going to have to ask them to leave. Either scenario is painful. There's pain involved in creating a brand that can withstand crisis, and you have to be willing to do it.

Can you do this on your own? Definitely. Many brands have. I say go for it. Give it a whirl. Be the best you can.

I've provided everything you need. I wrote two books, and I gave the methodology away practically for free.

But if the challenge seems greater than what you think your team can handle, or if you just don't have the bandwidth, we're here to help. I've built an entire agency that is designed around doing this at a very high level. We can partner with your organization and lead you through the process.

In fact, I believe so much in the transformative power of what I do, I'll make you this offer. Hire me, pay me nothing up front, and after you experience the value I bring in terms of the long-term success of your business, opening up new financial territory, and streamlining your branding by focusing on that ideal customer, then you can assess the impact and pay me whatever you think it's worth.

I proudly and confidently make that offer. I hope you'll take me up on it.

Thanks for reading my book. Also, please check out *Branding Is Sex*, which clearly lays out the how-to of brand strategy.

Drop me a note and let me know how your branding is going.

Sincerely,

Deb

ACKNOWLEDGMENTS

Thank you to the clients, employees, and friends of Sol Marketing who indulge my obsession with making customers the heroes of their own stories through the practice of branding. The Sol Sunbeams and I are on track to create $1B of brand value by 2025.

I am grateful for my publishing team and Scribe Media, especially my editor, Chris Balish, with whom it seems I share a brain. For the second time, Chris expertly nailed my voice and point of view and gave life to my ideas in a manuscript that reads like I'm sitting right next to the reader.

I am also grateful for the guidance of my executive coach and confidant, Andrew Blickstein, who encouraged me to own the idea of "irrational loyalty." And on that note,

I'd like to thank my friend Tucker Max, without whom this book would have been called something really stupid.

Because writing a book is super f—ing hard and sometimes keeps you from some of the lighter and, frankly, more fun aspects of life, I need to thank everyone in my "tribe" who endured my hesitation to commit to get-togethers and outings and who tirelessly listened to me obsess about story ideas, chapter titles, and precisely which dog would make it onto this book's cover.

For her unconditional love, and for at least acting like she understands what I'm talking about when I obsess about the latest corporate brand screw-up, I send gratitude Hannah McEvilly's way. As my only offspring, perhaps she feels obligated to support me. I admire her for doing so in her own irrationally loyal way. (Mommy's sorry about putting the words "awesome" and "Mommy" on moratorium when you were eight.)

Finally, I need to extend a hearty thanks to my publicity team of Janet Shapiro and Erin McDonald-Birnbaum at Smith Publicity, whose intrepid media relations skills nudged me into hundreds of conversations about brands gone wild, letting me always have the last word on how brands can build a foundation that allows them to thrive in the most tumultuous times.

ABOUT THE AUTHOR

DEB GABOR is the founder of Sol Marketing, a consultancy that has led successful strategy engagements since 2003 for global brands like Dell, Microsoft, and NBCUniversal, and for numerous digital brands, including Allrecipes, Cheezburger, HomeAway, and many more. A leading expert on brand disasters, she is the author of *Branding Is Sex: Get Your Customers Laid and Sell the Hell out of Anything*, and she has been featured in *USA Today* and other major publications. A displaced midwesterner, Deb currently lives in Austin, Texas, but travels frequently to help her clients build bulletproof brands.

Made in the USA
Las Vegas, NV
27 May 2021

23766149R00100